This is a deep and exciting book. It focuses on synodality and draws you in with its simple charm and use of vivid images from ordinary life experiences. It invites us to understand synodality from different angles; a judicious use of contending images – aloneness and togetherness, silence and myriad voices, observation and reflection. I particularly like the use of metaphors from nature that remind us that synodality is about listening and learning from the earth too. These very fine daily meditations will indeed slow us down and help us discover together the extraordinary in the ordinary.

Fr. Martin Sirju, Vicar General,
Archdiocese of Port of Spain, Trinidad and Tobago

Thanks to these trailblazing experts in charting the way towards being a synodal Church. Born from the experiences of authentic Caribbean people, it is a potpourri of faith-based reflection, creativity, empathy, and grace that doesn't pretend to neatly package the answers to some difficult questions, but rather, empowers people with tools to be transformative agents in the Church's conversion and mission. This work meets people where they're at and journeys with them as they recognise the presence of the Holy Spirit in their lives. You don't need to be a religious specialist to appreciate this book. It deservedly earns itself the title, "truly Catholic", and is like an appetising, costly spice that adds impressive flavour to the blessed fruits of our great Christian tradition.

Angelo Kurbanali
Youth Ministry collaborator, Trinidad and Tobago

Dis long time gal mi neva si yuh, come mek wi walk an talk.

As the Church gathers for the synodal journey, there are moments where many people would not have seen or heard from each other, as this line from a traditional Jamaican song acutely expresses. But here is presented an opportunity for you to listen to each other on an intentional journey. In this book, you experience a Church that is being called to pay attention to the other; none shall be left behind. These reflections are timely and crucial as the Church participates in a vastly changing and fluid world. For the ministers of today to be relevant, they need to use this book as a guide as they journey towards a synodical Church.

Fr. Richard Brown
Pastor, Stella Maris Roman Catholic Church,
Archdiocese of Kingston, Jamaica

Synodality is meant to be lived. Any practical guidance on its living faithfully among the faithful is welcome. This is an easy-to-read highly practical guide filled with vivid imagery, honest and thought-provoking, bite-size reflections, deeply rooted in the experience of the Caribbean Catholic Church. It is accompanied by stimulating exercises and challenges to deepen learning and action towards a more synodal Church. Listen to the voice of a priest-pastor-administrator-scholar and an Emotional and Spiritual Intelligence coach as they share exercises for personal, familial, and pastoral growth into discernment as we answer the synodal call to walk together in faith. Be stirred by synodality as life-giving intercourse and chastened by the imperfections of our walk. Prepare to engage a year long, one-a-day journey guided by the Spirit.

Anna Kasafi Perkins
Adjunct Faculty,
St. Michael's Theological College, Jamaica

WALKING TOGETHER

CARIBBEAN REFLECTIONS ON THE SYNODAL JOURNEY

DONALD D. CHAMBERS &
JUDY JOSEPH McSWEEN

Walking Together:
Caribbean Reflections on The Synodal Journey

Copyright © 2024
Donald D. Chambers & Judy Joseph McSween
All Rights Reserved

No part of this book may be reproduced or transmitted in any form or by any means, electronically or by photocopying or otherwise, without prior written permission from the author, except by a reviewer, who may quote brief passages in a review.

Cover design and layout Renee M. Simeon

This book is dedicated to the Most Rev. Edgerton Roland Clarke, Archbishop Emeritus of Kingston, Jamaica. As a seminarian and priest, I recall many of your homilies were grounded in the theme of communion. In our recent conversations, you made the nexus between Vatican II and the Synod journey when you said:

Communion is fellowship, openness to reaching out, reconciliation; to have an open door to welcome people, reconcile and unite them to Christ who presents them to the Father. In baptism, we are grafted to Christ and the Church; through Christ, we are one with Christ and each other. Therefore, the Church is communion. If there is no communion, there is no Church.

SYNOD PRAYER

We stand before You, Holy Spirit,
as we gather together in Your name.
With You alone to guide us,
make Yourself at home in our hearts.
Teach us the way we must go
and how we are to pursue it.
We are weak and sinful;
do not let us promote disorder.
Do not let ignorance lead us down the wrong path
nor partiality influence our actions.
Let us find in You our unity
so that we may journey together to eternal life
and not stray from the way of truth and what is right.
All this we ask of You,
who are at work in every place and time,
in the communion of the Father and the Son,
forever and ever. Amen.

Table of Contents

Acknowledgements	xvii
Foreword	xxi
Introduction	1
Guidelines for Working in Groups & Personal Reflection	7
What is Discernment? An Introduction	11
1. Communion, Participation, and Mission	17
2. Synod and the Caribbean Presence	21
3. Spirit Driven	27
4. Synod: A Bitter Pill	33
5. The Word "Synod"	39
6. Synod and the Unknown	43
7. Synod and Preparation	49
8. The Aged	55
9. Ecclesial Bunkers	59

10.	Walking Together	63
11.	Home Garden: Imperfect Icon of Synodality	67
12.	Synodal Waves	71
13.	Synodality and Lent	75
14.	Temptations as Pitfalls (First Sunday of Lent, Year C – Luke 4:1-13)	79
15.	Transfiguration Moments (Second Sunday of Lent, Year C – Luke 9:28-36)	83
16.	Priestly Anniversary Gift	87
17.	Building a Synodal Church	91
18.	A Graced Journey	95
19.	Dialectic	99
20.	Human Family	103
21.	Leadership	107
22.	Synodality and Catechesis	111
23.	Synodality and Conversations	117
24.	Synodality and the Holy Spirit	123
25.	Conversion and Evangelisation	129
26.	Listen, Build Bridges	135
27.	Synod as Listening	141
28.	Historical Listening and Kairos	147
29.	Listening to the Other	151
30.	Reception of Ideas	157
31.	Bridle & Bit Discipline	161
32.	Synodal Eyes	165
33.	Synod as Storytelling	169

TABLE OF CONTENTS

34. Synod Response	175
35. Waiting	181
36. Conflict Transformation	185
37. Frustration	189
38. Solitude	193
39. Contributing to the Whole	197
40. Conversion	201
41. Ego	205
42. Dance of the Kairos and Chronos	209
43. Synod Thoughts: Pope Francis & Brené Brown	213
44. Jigsaw Puzzle: Metaphor for the Synodal Journey	217
45. Synod Journey to Matelot	221
46. Synodality Lesson at the Swimming Pool	225
47. Community	229
48. Synodality in Action	233
49. A Taste of Perfection, Satisfaction, and Completeness	237
50. Imperfections	241
51. An Anthropological & Psychological Take on Synodality	245
52. Togetherness	249
Conclusion	253
Works Cited & Consulted	257
About the Authors	265

Acknowledgements

I start by thanking friends, family members, colleagues, brother priests, religious sisters, acquaintances, strangers, and parishioners. My writings are inspired by ordinary encounters with them, which form the raw material through which I encounter the incarnate God, Jesus Christ.

The idea for the book erupted from a conversation with Anna Kasafi Perkins, who has published several chapters and books on Christian ethics and Caribbean theology. She believes that more Caribbean authors ought to contribute to the reservoir of global and regional ideas shaped by our perspectives. We also discussed publishing my blogs and articles on the synod, accompanied by searching questions to assist the People of God in understanding and integrating synodality as a way of life. I am grateful that she also agreed to write an endorsement for this publication.

Judy Joseph McSween, with her skills in the twin Spiritual and Emotional Intelligence disciplines, agreed to co-author this project with me. Her formation work with clergy and laity across religious and denominational boundaries throughout the Caribbean prepared her to design the "Synodal Exercise" sections in the book. These are intended to encourage readers to integrate the material into their lives and assist them in living out their Christian vocations.

The Most Reverend Dr. Charles Jason Gordon, Archbishop of Port of Spain, wrote the foreword to this book, having recently published his own book on synodality, *Reviving Our Caribbean Soul: A Contemplative Synodal Journey*. His proactive and assertive approach to promoting the synodal journey regionally and locally makes him ideal for assessing the value of this publication to the growth of the Caribbean Church.

I am grateful to Fr. Peter McIsaac, S.J., Director of Synodal Transformation in the Archdiocese of Port of Spain, for reviewing the manuscript and giving constructive feedback. I appreciate his contribution to this project's theme of discernment; his article insightfully illustrates the value of attentiveness to the Holy Spirit. Fr. Peter's involvement indicates the value he sees in this project for synodal formation in the dioceses of the Caribbean.

Rachael Mair-Boxill and Marcia Ormsby initially edited and critiqued most of my blogs and articles, converting my raw insights into readable form. I am indebted to Lauren Branker who designs and manages my blog, *belovedreflections.org*. Lauren also edits, designs, and uploads the blogs and articles

ACKNOWLEDGEMENTS

with her unique style of critique. As Communications Officer of the Antilles Episcopal Conference, she frequently circulates the synod articles to regional Catholic media, making them accessible to a broader readership.

My thanks to Raymond Syms, editor of the *Catholic News* of the Archdiocese of Port of Spain, who has always graciously published my articles in the paper's print and online issues.

Book publication is only possible with the keen eyes of a professional and relatable editor. At my first introduction to and meeting with Laura Ann Phillips, there was clear evidence that she was a suitable editor for this book. Her eye for detail, knowledge of editing skills, religious commitment, and wearing the reader's shoes were a valuable addition to this project.

Equally, Renee Simeon, the graphic designer of both the inside and outside of the book, became the pilot, allowing the aeroplane of publication to take off safely and in refined style. Her knowledge of book publication and what the reader is attracted to has been invaluable.

This work is intended primarily for the person in the pew, so the feedback of those working in the pastoral trenches was essential. I am, therefore, grateful to Fr. Martin Sirju, rector of the Cathedral of the Immaculate Conception, Port of Spain, Fr. Richard Brown, pastor of the Stella Maris Church, Archdiocese of Kingston, Jamaica, and Angelo Kurbunali, a young theologian active in youth and assorted ministries in the Archdiocese of Port of Spain, for reading the manuscript and their public endorsement of the book.

Finally, I am appreciative of you, the reader. This project has taken off owing to our walking together; you are my inspiration. I look forward to your feedback, which I will certainly consider for future books.

Foreword

In the pages that follow, you will embark on a journey – a synodal journey. This journey is a spiritual odyssey that traverses the landscapes of faith, doubt, transformation, and mission. It's a journey prompted by the winds of change blowing through the corridors of the Church, beckoning its members to listen, discern, and respond to the whispers of the Holy Spirit.

As we delve into the depths of this text, we find ourselves confronted with the stark realities of our times. The narrative unfolds against the backdrop of a world grappling with uncertainty, upheaval, and disillusionment. The Covid-19 pandemic, like an uninvited guest, disrupted the rhythms of our lives, shaking the very foundations of our faith communities. It laid bare the vulnerabilities and shortcomings of the Church, exposing fissures that had long remained concealed.

But within these challenges lies an invitation – an invitation to reimagine, to recalibrate, and to rediscover the essence of our calling as disciples of Christ. This book is a testament to that invitation, a clarion call to embrace a new paradigm of being Church, one that is rooted in synodality, communion, and mission.

At its core, this text is a mosaic woven from the threads of lived experiences, theological reflections, and pastoral insights. It is a tapestry that draws upon the wisdom of Scripture, the teachings of the Magisterium, and the riches of Tradition. But woven into this tapestry are also the vibrant hues of contemporary Caribbean voices – voices that echo the joys and struggles, the hopes and fears of believers navigating the complexities of the present age.

The journey begins with an honest appraisal of the challenges facing the Church in the wake of the pandemic. We are confronted with the stark reality of dwindling participation, frayed communal bonds, and a sense of alienation that has seeped into the fabric of our ecclesial communities. But even amidst this gloom, there are glimmers of hope, signs of resilience, creativity, and adaptability that testify to the enduring vitality of the Church.

Central to this narrative is the concept of synodality, a term that may seem unfamiliar to some but resonates deeply with the ethos of our faith. Synodality is more than just a buzzword, it is a spiritual disposition, a way of being Church that is inclusive, participatory, and discerning. It calls us to journey together, to listen attentively to one another and to the promptings of the Spirit as we seek to discern God's will for His people.

FOREWORD

As we traverse the terrain of synodality, we encounter a cast of characters – pastors, theologians, lay faithful – who share their insights and experiences, their struggles and triumphs on the road to a more synodal Church. We hear the voices of youth leaders lamenting the loss of a generation, of theologians challenging us to broaden our horizons, of catechists illuminating the path of faith formation.

But this journey is not merely an intellectual exercise; it is an invitation to conversion, a call to encounter Christ anew, and to allow His transformative love to penetrate every aspect of our lives. We are reminded that true conversion is more than just a change of heart; it is a change of direction, a reorientation of our lives towards the person of Jesus Christ.

In the chapters that follow, we explore the intersection of synodality with key dimensions of ecclesial life – catechesis, liturgy, evangelisation – illuminating how this ancient concept breathes new life into age-old practices. We are invited to reimagine catechesis as a journey of faith shared by the entire community, to rediscover the richness of the liturgy as the source and summit of our worship, to embrace evangelisation as a mission shared by all the baptised.

But perhaps the most poignant moments of this journey are those of transfiguration, those moments of encounter with the divine that leave us forever changed. We are reminded that our journey is not one of despair but of hope, not of darkness but of light. It is a journey that culminates in the joy of Easter, the triumph of life over death, of love over fear.

As we embark on this synodal journey together, may we be inspired by the witness of the saints who have gone before us, men and women who, in every age, have borne witness to the transformative power of the Gospel. And may we, like them, be bold and courageous in our response to the Spirit's call, trusting that He who has begun a good work in us will bring it to completion.

In the end, this book is more than just a collection of words on a page. It is an invitation, a summons, to embrace the journey, to walk together in faith and communion, and to be transformed by the renewing power of the Holy Spirit. May it be a source of inspiration, encouragement, and renewal for all who embark on this synodal pilgrimage.

I invite you to engage this book and allow its insights to challenge you to deepen your discipleship and grow your love for God and each other. The authors have modelled for us the value of collaboration between a priest, Fr. Donald Chambers, and a lay person, Judy Joseph McSween, in offering us a synodal pathway. This is a great witness to the value of synodality as the People of God walking together to listen, dialogue, and discern.

+ Most Rev. Dr. Charles Jason Gordon
Archbishop of Port of Spain

Introduction

The Synod 2021-2024 was launched by Pope Francis on October 10, 2021, with the theme, "For a Synodal Church: Communion, Participation, and Mission." A synodal Church means that the laity, religious, and clergy, identified as the People of God in communion with God and each other, actively participate in the mission of the Church to "make disciples of all nations" (Matthew 28:19).

The aim of the synod is to form the Church so that we learn to "walk together" as both a *modus vivendi*, a way of living as Church, and a *modus operandi*, a way of working as Church.

The synodal journey involves discerning the way in which God calls the Church to exercise its missionary mandate in the twenty-first century.

Each historical epoch has its own unique questions and concerns. The Good News of Jesus Christ must, therefore, be packaged according to the needs of each historical period. In the first century, for example, the Early Church consisted of Gentiles and Jews. A question pertinent to them was whether Jewish religious rituals, particularly circumcision, should be applied to the Gentiles. Consequently, representatives of various Christian communities gathered in Jerusalem to discern the voice of the Spirit in this regard (Acts 15).

From the birth of the Church, "walking together" has been at the core of her missionary impulse. Consider the cultural, ideological, ethnic, geographic, spiritual, intellectual, social, and demographic diversity that exists in the Body of Christ. Discerning God's will, therefore, is a challenging and difficult task. To "walk together" consists of an awareness of the tensions arising from this diversity and learning to sense the voice of the Holy Spirit in these tensions.

The synod logo offers insight into the nature of "walking together" in diversity. It features persons of varying ages, religious status, and physical capacities, each with their particular interests, needs, questions, and cultural backgrounds. To discern the Holy Spirit's voice, the journey invites participants to <u>listen</u> to each other and to the Word of God as they engage in conversation with each other, with persons in their own communities, and those living on the periphery of society.

This listening must encompass respecting moments of silence, creating space for expressions of raw emotion, and receiving these compassionately. We are called to respect similar perspectives, while remaining open to differing views. The voices of youth, the aged, and the sick ought to be given priority.

INTRODUCTION

To discern the voice of the Holy Spirit among divergent perspectives, the Church, in her wisdom, has been aware of the value of dialogue between the *sensus fidei* (sense of the faithful/People of God) and the Magisterium, or teaching function of the pastors. This dialogue can lead to the state where a "unanimous consensus of the whole Church in the same faith is realised" (*Preparatory Document* #14).

The bishops' discernment of the Spirit consists of listening to the People of God (*Lumen Gentium* #12). Relying on the guidance and direction of the Holy Spirit, the Church is mindful that the Spirit prepares us to "walk together" by equipping and empowering us with human skills. One such skill is emotional intelligence: the ability to be aware of and manage emotions in order to build human relationships.

Someone once shared with me: "I left the private sector to work in the Church full-time, thinking it [would be] a more loving, merciful, and compassionate environment. After one year, I escaped, totally disappointed."

On a separate occasion, another person said, "I don't wish to get involved in Church committees. I will give my financial contribution. Too much backstabbing and bacchanal!"

"Why?" I inquired.

"After facing conflicts, infighting, competition, and undermining behaviour at work, I come to Church for solace, but what greets me is the same behaviour. I stay far."

What's happening in these two circumstances? Think of the four legs of a chair. Imagine that each leg represents one aspect of the human person; there are human (physical and emotional), spiritual, intellectual, and social, or communal, elements. Now, imagine that one or two legs are weaker than the others, and a heavyset person sits. You don't need to stretch your imagination to figure out the results. To withstand such a heavy weight, each leg must be of equal strength.

The missing piece of the puzzle may be human formation, specifically, in emotional intelligence, the primary ingredient for human relationships. Emotional intelligence is being aware of and managing our feelings by marrying them with reasoning.

Mature emotional intelligence enables us to develop the skills to forge quality human relationships. St. Thomas Aquinas writes: "Grace builds upon nature." Imagine you have a bucket with several holes, and you pour water, or grace, into it. Naturally, the water escapes. Deficient human formation is like a bucket with holes.

Embarking on this synodal journey, the Holy Spirit invites the Church to experience continuing human and spiritual formation and conversion. This involves allowing the Holy Spirit to change our mindset and heart as a means towards openness to discerning God's voice. This book is a collaborative effort in synodal spirit between Judy Joseph McSween and I. Our intention is to offer opportunities for reflection and exercises to assist in the spiritual and human formation of the People of God, enabling them to sharpen their skills of discernment.

Each chapter presents a synod reflection from my blog site, *belovedreflections.org,* and articles published in the *Catholic News*, a newspaper produced by Catholic Media

INTRODUCTION

Services Limited (CAMSEL). This is the communications arm of the Archdiocese of Port of Spain.

At the end of each chapter, there is a "Missionary Challenge" that captures core themes. A "Synodal Exercise" follows, in which Judy's prayerfully crafted questions invite you to reflection, whether you're making this journey alone, with your family, or with a parish ministry. There are fifty-two chapters in all; we recommend contemplating one each week.

Fr. Peter McIsaac, S.J., explores the fundamentals of deepening our awareness of the interior movements of the Holy Spirit in a guest article entitled, "What is Discernment? An Introduction." This piece is an invaluable guide to the process of discernment as we seek to encounter and unite ourselves to this God whom we long to know, love, and serve.

The focus on synodality emphasises the discernment of God's will by the community. Thus, this book also helps the reader to develop their own personal discernment skills, realising that personal discernment enriches communal discernment. In writing about the steps in community discernment, Jesuit Superior, Arturo Sosa, notes that the group gathered for communal discernment, knowing God's will for the community, ought to be the right persons who can listen to the Spirit in their own lives. "If they are not open individually," he says, "they probably will not be able to be much open to discernment in common." The reflections of this book aim to assist both personal and community discernment.

I pray this book becomes a valuable formation tool that equips us, as part of the Church, for walking together and discerning the movement of the Holy Spirit as the Church missions in the twenty-first century.

Fr. Donald D. Chambers

Guidelines for Working in Groups & Personal Reflection

Groups can be holy spaces for reflection, discussion, and discernment. Both facilitators and group members have their respective roles in creating these.

GUIDELINES

Facilitators are asked to acknowledge, to self and to participants, that the space being used for these reflections is a sacred space. You are encouraged to welcome the Holy Spirit and pray that the Spirit's presence be manifest to all. Seek God's guidance as you facilitate group members' introspection and sharing. Your prayer and disposition ought to reflect the precept: "Thy will be done" (Matthew 6:10). To effectively fulfil your role as group facilitator, you should:

1. Familiarise yourself with the reflection process.
2. Be fully present.

3. Ensure ground rules for the group are kept as per the Group Member Guidelines (see below).
4. Facilitate the process, rather than participate.
5. Keep the group focussed and on track with regard to content and time.
6. Listen carefully and actively to the discussion.
7. Manage the discussion effectively, allowing for inclusion of all group members and balanced use of airtime.
8. Remain neutral; avoid jumping to conclusions or making assumptions.
9. Pay attention to nonverbal cues such as body language and tone of voice.
10. Allow space between contributions to hear how the Holy Spirit may be guiding the group.
11. Schedule timely breaks.
12. Create and maintain a safe and open environment for sharing ideas.

GROUP MEMBER GUIDELINES

Group members are encouraged to:

1. Practise active listening.
2. Be curious.
3. Observe the "One voice" rule; have only one person speak at a time.
4. Personalise your contributions by using "I" rather than "we".

5. Respect the facilitator, each participant, and their views.
6. Be fully present to the group and the exercise.

PERSONAL REFLECTION GUIDELINES

If you would like to use the material in this book for your personal reflection, we encourage you to:

1. Identify a quiet space – a "me" space – to which you will retreat for your reflections. Ensure that this area is free of anything which may distract you.
2. Prepare for your reflection by silencing yourself, letting go of distracting thoughts or pains and becoming fully present. Pray for the Holy Spirit's guidance.
3. Focus on only one chapter per session.
4. End the session as you began (see point 2) – with quiet time in which you can hear what else the Holy Spirit may wish to say.

What is Discernment?
An Introduction

For sixty years, the Church has promoted the full and active participation of the laity. This has had a profound effect on the way we celebrate our liturgies and transformed how we have worked together to organise our mission and communities. We have parish councils, finance committees, commissions, and ministry animation teams. Team building and partnership have become important ways to exercise our service of God's people, uniting the community of the Church as a single "body".

Today, the call to genuine "synodality" is really a deepening of that process which began many decades ago. It transforms the way every member participates in the life and mission of the Church, offering a means of discerning the will of God for us. Discernment, then, is at the centre of the synod process.

At every level of the Church, from local communities to the gathering in Rome, we are invited to have "Conversations in the Spirit". A Conversation in the Spirit is a fundamental form of what we would call "communal discernment".

What are some of the fundamental principles of discernment? The first and most important principle is that it is a form of prayer. We enter the process of discernment seeking to encounter God, to deepen our awareness of the presence of the Holy Spirit, and to unite ourselves to God so that we might know, love, and serve the Lord.

The focus of genuine discernment, then, is this encounter. We are not coming together to advance a personal agenda or simply to "brainstorm," so that we come up with an intelligent plan that has the support of the majority. We are discerning God's will through the genuine attentiveness that comes from prayerful listening and speaking. To be open to this will of God, we must be aware of our own biases and preferences. Discernment means we are willing to detach ourselves, as much as we are able, from our self-centredness and our desire to control the outcome.

A second important principle is that discernment takes time, patience, and much practice. This flows out of the first principle; our awareness of God and our union with Him is itself the gift of the Spirit. We do not deserve or earn God's grace. It is a free gift. How and when the Spirit moves us is not something we can control or exploit, no matter how effective our processes are or how good our intentions may be. We must be willing to listen attentively to our God who speaks in the depths of our hearts and in the community of disciples.

Becoming familiar with how God speaks to us and the effect God's presence has upon us requires the regular discipline of prayer. An important practice in this regard is "review". I review my prayer when I have finished to see how God has touched me. I review my day to see when, where, and how God has been present to me in my activities and relationships; we call this form of discernment an "Examen of Consciousness". I may also take time to review important meetings or conversations to discern how God was at work in those interactions. In a "Conversation in the Spirit", this review involves pondering and discerning the movement of the Spirit.

A third, and important, principle is that it is sometimes difficult to discern how God is moving us in prayer and in our Conversations in the Spirit. I can be deceived, distracted, and confused by what I experience. It is useful, then, to have a spiritual director who is skilled in the practice of discernment to help me understand my prayer. In the same way, it is important that a Conversation in the Spirit has someone who is skilled in discernment to help guide the conversation, and help the group recognise important moments of consolation and desolation in the process.

What are we looking for in our personal and communal discernment processes? As I mentioned, any genuine discernment process seeks to encounter, to deepen our awareness, and unite ourselves to our God.

God is love. That means our experience of God is an experience of divine love. But how does that divine love – which is beyond our images, ideas, feelings – become part of our human experience? Here, we are really asking: how am I moved by this experience? There may be emotions, insights, and desires that surface in my prayer, but how do I discern whether these are of God or if I am merely deceived?

We often speak of consolation and desolation as a means of discerning God's presence and will. Our images, emotions, desires, and insights are understood and judged, then, according to divine love. Does my experience lead me to greater faith, hope, and love, or does it lead me to a lack of trust, a sense of hopelessness and self-centredness?

There are impulses of the human spirit that we can identify as inner movements of divine love, which are good indicators of God's loving presence. Contrition (sorrow for wounding my beloved), gratitude (appreciation of the gifts of the beloved), and compassion (union with the other) are good examples; these are rarely deceptive. They open for us the mystery of God's love, as well as the fullness of our humanity, the purpose for which we were created. They inspire in us humility – really reverence for God – as well as a sense of awe for the beauty, truth, and goodness of God.

What do these interior movements look like in a discernment process of the community? The obvious signs of consolation in community emerge as harmony and consensus, expressing in some way the sense of contrition (the desire for reconciliation), gratitude for the diversity of gifts in the community, and compassion: the unitive power of God in the community.

Just as consolation is discerned on the personal level by a movement of divine love, so love expresses itself as consensus and harmony in the community. It opens itself to others (inclusivity) through sacred listening and speaking (dialogue). It is the unifying work of the Spirit, who is Love.

WHAT IS DISCERNMENT?

On occasion, though, there are prophetic voices, those "on the margins", that speak to the community beyond the harmony and consensus that binds us as a body. We are always in need of reform, and these voices open us to the creative power of God's love. So, while we look for the love that binds us through harmony and consensus, we also open ourselves to the creative and transformative power of the Spirit, who speaks to us from "the margins".

What are the fruits of consensus? As we review our Conversation in the Spirit, we discern the movements of consolation and desolation, but we are also attentive to the fruits of the process. These may be recognised as:

- Deepening communion through the graces of reconciliation and healing.
- An increase of our commitment to the process, in spite of the sacrifices and challenges.
- A sense of peace with the outcome, even when differences of opinion remain.
- A clearer sense of identity and mission.
- The possible emergence of priorities for ministry at the local level, the elements of a pastoral plan at the level of a diocese, and animating principles for the universal Church.

Discernment is simply attentiveness to and awareness of God in our prayer, our daily activities, and our diverse networks of relationships. It is given to us as a gift of the Spirit, but we are called to cultivate the gift through regular practice and guidance of others. The more we engage the attentiveness of discernment, the deeper our awareness of

God will become in all things, transforming all dimensions of our life, community, and ministry.

Fr. Peter McIsaac, S.J.
Director of Synodal Transformation
Archdiocese of Port of Spain

CHAPTER ONE

Communion, Participation, and Mission

> [T]he temptation to treat the Synod as a kind of a parliament...confuses synodality with a "political battle" in which, in order to govern, one side must defeat the other.
> *(Handbook for the Synod on Synodality)*

The theme of the Catholic Church's Synod on Synodality is, "For a Synodal Church: Communion, Participation, and Mission." In **communion** with Jesus Christ, disciples participate together in a journey of listening to the Holy Spirit and to each other. In so doing, we learn to discern what the Holy Spirit says to the Church and to the world about the Church's mission.

Pope Francis invited all baptised persons, ecumenical and interreligious groups, the society, and persons on the margins of the Church to participate by speaking openly and listening. Dioceses worldwide, in regions such as those within the

Antilles Episcopal Conference, practised listening to discern the voice of the Holy Spirit. These exercises culminated in a gathering of bishops in October 2023.

The purpose of the synod is:

> [T]o plant dreams, draw forth prophecies and visions, allow hope to flourish, inspire trust, bind up wounds, weave together relationships, awaken a dawn of hope, learn from one another and create a bright resourcefulness that will enlighten minds, warm hearts, give strength to our hands. (*Preparatory Document #32*)

To avoid the synod adopting a parliament-like spirit, the process is guided by these practices:

- Communal prayer.
- Reflections on the word of God, with questions related to themes such as listening, speaking out, and sharing responsibility for our common mission.
- Dialogue in Church and society.

This synodal journey, and Pope Francis in particular, has encountered criticism. In a September 2019 article in the Jesuit magazine, *America*, Victor Codina, S.J., says that opposition to Francis stems from the fact that he is from the "Global South" – Argentina, to be exact – and is not a theologian. He says some of Francis' detractors believe that the pope's "deficit in theology would explain his dangerous positions on God's mercy [in his 2015 papal bull] 'Misericordiae Vultus'". Others consider the pope's position on mercy "scandalous because it lessens the grace and cross of Jesus".

Codina rebuts these views. He says that although Pope Francis "studied and taught pastoral theology at San Miguel de Buenos Aires" in Argentina, he now "does not aspire to fulfil [his papal] role as a theologian but as a pastor". He adds: "What really bothers his detractors is that his theology stems from the reality of injustice, poverty and the destruction of nature, and from the reality of ecclesial clericalism."

For this reason, there is a focus on discerning the voice of the Holy Spirit as the Church traverses and missions in today's world. Pope Francis dreams of an inclusive synodal journey that returns to the spirit of consultation and discernment we see at the Council of Jerusalem (Acts 15). At this council, three groups of persons are offered opportunities to speak and listen before a decision is made on the matter of circumcising Gentile converts: Paul and Barnabas, Peter, and the members of the Pharisee party.

In the mission of the Church, the synod does not make the parliamentary method the *modus vivendi et operandi* – the way of living and working. Rather, it aims to place listening to discern at the heart of the Church's missionary journey.

Individual or Group Reflection

MISSIONARY CHALLENGE

In **communion** with Jesus Christ, disciples **participate** together in a journey of listening to the Holy Spirit and to each other. In so doing, we learn to discern what the Holy Spirit says to the Church and to the world about the Church's **mission**.

SYNODAL EXERCISE

1. Reflect on a moment when you have experienced yourself truly listening to the Holy Spirit.
2. Recall a time when you believed you really listened fully to what a family member, a friend, or even a stranger may have been saying. What were the circumstances that allowed you to give your full attention to the other?
3. In your next conversation, observe what happens when you attempt to listen attentively to the other person and when you seek to discern God's presence in the interaction.

CHAPTER TWO

Synod and The Caribbean Presence

The synodal journey began with the diocesan and continental phases, climaxing with the meeting of bishops in October 2023. We completed the diocesan phase with a regional synthesis. In August 2022, Cardinal Mario Grech, the synod president, reported that the secretariat had received one hundred and three syntheses from one hundred and fourteen episcopal conferences.

The continental phase began in October 2022. The Antilles Episcopal Conference, the assembly of Caribbean bishops, belongs to the continental group of Latin America and the Caribbean and to the sub-group of the Caribbean, which includes Cuba, Haiti, the Dominican Republic, and Puerto Rico. The dialogue at the continental level was guided by the various syntheses from the continental group's member territories. At the end of that dialogue, a synthesis from our continental phase was submitted along with syntheses from the remaining five continents of North America, Europe, Africa, Asia, and Oceania.

Synod is an old tradition of the Church. It indicates the journey on which the People of God – laity, clergy, bishops – walk together in its mission. It also refers to Jesus Christ, who is "the Way, the Truth, and the Life" (John 14:6). Therefore, disciples of Jesus are followers of the Way – followers of Jesus (Acts 9:2).

The origin of the word "synod" is a composite of two Greek words: *sun*, meaning "together", and *hodos*, meaning "way". A synod is not just a meeting or an event. A synod refers to the People of God journeying in **communion** with Christ, listening to the Holy Spirit and the Word of God, and **participating** together in the **mission** of the Church.

By virtue of our baptism, we are called to participate fully in the life and mission of the Church: "Go, therefore, make disciples of all nations…" (Matthew 28:19). While the Good News of Jesus Christ remains constant, the way in which the Church packages the message changes depending on historical circumstances and cultures. This is referred to as the "signs of the times" (*Free*). To read and discern the "signs of the times", we listen to each other and to the Word of God to respond to the question: How is the Holy Spirit guiding and directing the Church's mission today?

Perhaps you're tempted to wonder: why is my voice essential in the synodal journey? Picture for a moment a field of mango trees. The usefulness of the fruit depends on the growing and harvesting of several trees together that are nourished by unseen nutrients in the soil. Faith is this unseen nutrient that allows each person to respond to God's word. In communion, faith allows us to bear an abundance of fruits. Everyone's active faith is essential to producing a rich harvest.

You may also be wondering why the Church is speaking about a synodal journey at this time. Through continuing examination of conscience, the Church is aware of its own mismanagement of the mission of Jesus Christ, especially towards the weak and vulnerable, such as the victims of sexual abuse.

At the core of this failure is the historical dominance of the Church's "top-down" model of governance, a clerical and authoritarian mentality in which power and decision-making rests solely in the hands of priests and bishops. This mentality is an obstacle to discovering the Gospel, especially for weak and vulnerable persons – the voiceless ones, according to this model – at the lower end of the hierarchical ladder. Pope Francis, therefore, calls for a return to the model of the "People of God" journeying together and new governance structures which involve the People of God listening, discerning, and making decisions together.

Imagine two landmasses separated by a deep gorge. Now, employing a Freudian theory, consider one of the landmasses the "id", the human's most basic instinct, and the other, the "superego", or human morality. The bridge needed to connect the two is the "ego", or the reality.

The id says: "I am accustomed to making my own decisions. I can't depend on others." The superego responds: "But your decisions neglect our needs. We need to be listened to." In this circumstance, a mature "ego" bridge needs to be built to connect the two landmasses. We construct it by becoming aware of the current leadership instinct (id) and the moral voice (superego) that says: "This leadership instinct is unaligned to the Gospel of Jesus Christ."

To construct this ecclesial "ego" bridge, the People of God need to develop deeper awareness and listening skills to identify the spiritual and emotional materials needed to build it. Building this bridge, in religious language, is <u>conversion</u>. Conversion is the fruit of synodal journeying.

Individual or Group Reflection

MISSIONARY CHALLENGE

Conversion is the fruit of synodal journeying. Conversion is an interior transformation of a way of thinking in which I see myself, not as a single mango on a tree, but as one within a cluster of mangoes that contributes to a rich harvest.

SYNODAL EXERCISE

As you reflect on your synodal journey to date:

a. Have you observed the increased conversation among laity, clergy, and bishops? What emotions, if any, does this evoke in you?

b. Have you experienced Conversations in the Spirit – the People of God listening, discerning, and making decisions together?

c. Have you in any way experienced the deeper awareness and listening skills that accompany Conversations in the Spirit?

d. How might you become more deeply engaged in this conversion process?

> Let each of you look not only to his own interests, but also to the interests of others. Have this mind among yourselves, which is yours in Christ Jesus...
> (Philippians 2:4)

CHAPTER THREE

Spirit Driven

As I wrote the article that was this chapter's forerunner, many dioceses within the Antilles Episcopal Conference were undertaking the tedious task of the diocesan phase of the synodal journey. These dioceses ranged from Hamilton, Bermuda in the north to Belize City/Belmopan, Belize in the west, to Cayenne, French Guyana in the southeast.

In this first phase, parishes, lay movements, schools, universities, religious congregations, neighbourhood Christian communities, and social action, ecumenical, and inter-religious movements gathered to speak and listen, with intentionality, to each other and the Holy Spirit. The purpose was to discern what the Holy Spirit was saying to the Church.

These exercises, still so pertinent, were intended to "integrate the Synodal Process into the life of the local Church in creative ways that promote [deeper] communion, fuller participation, and a more fruitful mission" (*Vademecum* 3.1). In this listening phase, groups were encouraged "to gather and respond to stimulus questions/images/scenarios together, listen to each other, and provide individual and group feedback, ideas, reactions, and suggestions" (*Vademecum* 3.1). The questions served to generate discussion and stimulate deep, rich interaction, just as oil is used to lubricate mechanical engines.

As various groups gather today, they will encounter the diversity naturally found in a gathering of persons. They will find persons emotionally bruised from within or outside the Church needing a safe space to vent their emotions. They will meet persons whose raw and broken life circumstances trigger a kind of "dark night of the soul", a feeling of God's absence.

There will be persons holding hardened ideological positions who come to argue and reinforce what they consider to be orthodoxy. And then, there will be those who have abandoned the faith, uninterested in dialogue with the Church. The discussion may also be derailed from the guided questions track, leaving some discouraged and disheartened by the perceived non-achievement of goals.

If the group faces these or similar positions, what is the recommended action? First, participants ought not to react to volcanic emotional outbursts with pre-packaged platitudinal and religious formulas, such as those which Job's friend, Eliphaz, provides in response to Job's wounded story (Job 4). In *Job and the Mystery of Suffering*, Richard Rohr describes Eliphaz's advice as "agenda-driven" (p. 59). He adds:

"Ideology is a very common masquerade for real faith because the agenda looks good or religious" (p. 59).

While the synodal journey is stimulated by a structured agenda, we must remember it is Spirit-driven, as we pray in the first line of the Synod Prayer: "We stand before You, Holy Spirit, as we gather together in Your name."

What does a Spirit-driven process look like? In a social media chat, a colleague and friend of mine, Gloria Bertrand, offers an appropriate metaphor:

> Looking in your cupboard, seeing what you have, and making a meal out of it for the family to enjoy and be nourished. As against taking a recipe and looking for the ingredients far and wide, and then "bussing you head" to make a perfect dish that most people will not eat or enjoy, and therefore, remain hungry.

A Spirit-driven process pays close attention to the people who come on the journey with their own personal stories. The discussion questions serve as the vehicle enabling participants to speak boldly and courageously, and others to listen with intentionality. Participants ask open-ended questions that are not agenda-driven in order to enter and understand their experience. Should the discussion turn into a wild forest fire, the facilitator may invite participants to pause for a period of silence and ask themselves: "Based on my thoughts and feelings during the discussion, what is the Holy Spirit saying to me at this time?"

Jesus' conversation with the persistent Syrophoenician woman (Mark 7:24-30) demonstrates the value of courageous speaking and listening in the synodal journey. She demands to tell her story to Jesus and express her needs. Jesus' willingness to listen to her, notwithstanding His initial position to refuse her request, eventually evolves into a discernment of the Spirit: "For saying this, you may go."

Those who gather to speak must be bold and courageous. Listening must be intentional, despite the awkward, clumsy, or perhaps aggressive manner of expression.

The goal of the synod journey is not to establish a strategic plan with goals and objectives. This way of decision-making is based on the problem-solving approach. Pope Francis argues that listening and discernment of the Holy Spirit follows the example of Jesus. The discipline is, therefore, fundamental to the Church's mission.

If this way of being Church is new, awkward, or unclear, recall these words from the Synod Prayer: "Teach us the way we must go and how we are to pursue it." I invite you to direct these words to the Holy Spirit.

Individual or Group Reflection

MISSIONARY CHALLENGE

Pope Francis argues that listening and discernment of the Holy Spirit follows the example of Jesus. The discipline is, therefore, fundamental to the Church's mission.

If this way of being Church is new, awkward, or unclear, recall these words from the Synod Prayer: "Teach us the way we must go and how we are to pursue it." I invite you to direct these words to the Holy Spirit.

SYNODAL EXERCISE

1. Slowly read the Synod Prayer.
2. What phrase resonates with you?
3. Spend some time in prayerful reflection on the phrase. To what is the Holy Spirit inviting you?

SYNOD PRAYER

We stand before You, Holy Spirit,
as we gather together in Your name.
With You alone to guide us,
make Yourself at home in our hearts.
Teach us the way we must go
and how we are to pursue it.
We are weak and sinful;
do not let us promote disorder.
Do not let ignorance lead us down the wrong path
nor partiality influence our actions.
Let us find in You our unity
so that we may journey together to eternal life
and not stray from the way of truth and what is right.
All this we ask of You,
who are at work in every place and time,
in the communion of the Father and the Son,
forever and ever. Amen.

CHAPTER FOUR

Synod: A Bitter Pill

The Synod on Synodality is not an event. It is a journey of the People of God who listen to each other and the Holy Spirit to discern the movement of the Spirit in the life and mission of the Church. One of the characteristics of a journey – whether by foot, airplane, motor vehicle, or ship – is the element of surprise. The synod journey is no different; surprise is inherent in it.

This quality of surprise makes the synod journey a bitter pill for some to swallow. In this chapter, I rely on insights from Estelle Frankel's, *The Wisdom of Not Knowing*, to further understand the synod journey.

Jewish contemporary thinkers use the term "divine uncertainty principle" to describe God. The term is used to understand Moses' encounter with Yahweh in the account of the burning bush. When Moses asks to know Yahweh's name

(Exodus 3:14), he receives the response, "Ehyeh Asher Ehyeh", or "I Am Becoming as I Am Becoming".

This response suggests the free choice and unhindered power of God. While the root meaning of the name "Yahweh" is disputed, most scholars accept that it is a form of the verb "to be" and probably the causative form: "causes to be"; "create". Yahweh's response, therefore, indicates an indeterminate God, a Divine Becoming who will redeem the Israelites.

This answer suggests that Yahweh can neither be boxed in nor so clearly defined as a noun. If the root name for "God" is a verb and not a noun, then the Israelites are about to embark on a journey with a "Becoming God" who will surprise them. And indeed, they are surprised at the Sea of Reeds, in the desert, and on Mount Sinai.

Like all humans, Israel is tempted to make Yahweh into a noun or an idol (Exodus 32). An idol, which the molten calf is, "can be fully known in all its dimensions for it is finite and measurable, while the living God and Source of all being and becoming can never be known in its entirety" (p. 89).

We tend to seek certainty and reduce what is infinite to a finite state. Consequently, we often also tend to reduce God and God's activities:

> Instead of standing in the presence of mystery that is in a constant state of flux, ever changing and becoming, moment to moment, we seek to reduce God to a concept or ideas we can understand. (p. 80)

On their journey to Jerusalem, for example, Jesus takes Peter, James, and John to the mountain where there was a theophany – a revelation of God. Jesus is transfigured (Luke 9:28-36). Rather than stand in awe and wonder at God's revelation, Peter's creative suggestion of erecting three tents is an attempt to capture, or gift-wrap, the "Becoming God".

Frankel reminds us that the biblical metaphor for clinging to certainty, fixating on the past, and trying to control everything, is idolatry – the reduction of that which is infinite to something finite. It manifests in our extreme admiration and reverence for something, someone, or an idea.

She also points out that "our most authentic spiritual experiences can be turned into routinized religious ritual" (p. 80). A scriptural example of this is the Jewish Christians' attempt to subject Gentile converts to circumcision. Jewish mystic and theologian, Rav Kook, refers to it as turning the living God into an idol (p. 81), where we replace our direct experiential knowledge of God with our conceptual knowledge.

This occurs more frequently "in moments of anxiety or uncertainty when we seek comfort in old patterns and familiar habits, like the addict who reaches for his substance of choice when faced with stress and uncertainty" (p. 82). See why Pope Francis' synodal journey is a hard pill for some to swallow?

If the synod journey is being guided by the Spirit of the God of surprise, then we must be open to change and new possibilities. To listen, discuss, and pay attention to what the Spirit is saying requires conversion of heart and mind, that is, unlearning routine ways of sharing, listening, and discerning. Then, relearning new ways.

Pope Francis uses the metaphor of a pilgrim to demonstrate the importance of conversion in the synod journey. He says that a pilgrim is one who "goes out from herself, opens herself to a new horizon, and when she comes home she is no longer the same, and so her home won't be the same" (*Dream*, p. 135).

Those who refuse to relinquish their idols – routine ways of seeing God, thinking, and listening – will find the synod pill hard to swallow. Those who are open to encountering the "Becoming God" of surprise revealed in Jesus Christ will witness the fruits of the Holy Spirit in the "Promised Land".

Individual or Group Reflection

MISSIONARY CHALLENGE

If the synod journey is being guided by the Spirit of the God of surprise, then we must be open to change and new possibilities. To listen, discuss, and pay attention to what the Spirit is saying requires conversion of heart and mind, that is, unlearning routine ways of sharing, listening, and discerning. Then, relearning new ways.

SYNODAL EXERCISE

Prayer:

Change my heart and my mind, O God,
make them ever true.
Change my mind and heart, O God,
make me receptive to conversion.
Change my heart and my mind, O God,
may I be like You.
You are the potter, I am the clay,
Mold me and make me, this is what I pray.

Spend ten minutes in silence, just being in the presence of the Holy Spirit, listening.

CHAPTER FIVE

The Word "Synod"

Synod.
Five different, unique letters in relationship with each other.
Five letters that dance together, creating movement and meaning.
Letters that, together, mean a "common road".

Synod is:
    letters coming together to form words,

    words coming together to form sentences,

    sentences coming together to form paragraphs,

    paragraphs coming together to form chapters,

    chapters coming together to form stories,

    stories coming together to form books,

    books coming together to form libraries,

    libraries coming together to form collections of stories.

    All different, yet similar.

    Together, they tell the story of humanity,

the story of the Church.

Not my story.

Not the story of one race, religion, ethnicity, community, family, or nation.

Our story.

Synod.
A journey of one people,
each contributing his or her own letters, words, sentences, paragraphs, chapters, stories, books, and libraries.
Without one, the whole is unattainable.

Individual or Group Reflection

MISSIONARY CHALLENGE

Synod.

A journey of one people, each contributing his or her own letters, words, sentences, paragraphs, chapters, stories, books, and libraries.

Without one, the whole is unattainable.

SYNODAL EXERCISE

1. What will be your contribution to this synodal journey?
2. How might you actively participate in it?
3. How might you discern God's will?
4. How might you encourage others to participate?

CHAPTER SIX

Synod and the Unknown

> All journeys have a secret destination of which
> the traveller is unaware.
> (Martin Buber)

In this chapter, I reflect on the synod process as a journey of the unknown. Just as there was Covid-19 vaccine hesitancy, there exists a measure of synod hesitancy. Some battle-worn Church leaders are wary of the absence of clear goals.

Unlike previous synods, such as the New Evangelization (2012), Vocation and Mission of the Family (2014), Young People, the Faith and Vocational Discernment (2018), or the Pan-Amazon Region (2019), there is no thematic focus. It is a synod about the People of God journeying together to listen to each other and the Holy Spirit through a process of consultation – this is the focus. The hesitancy is fuelled by the unknown destination.

Have you ever had a hunch or an intuition to pursue a dream? Those who have acted upon these know, first-hand, that it begins with a journey towards an unknown destination. In *The Wisdom of Not Knowing*, author and spiritual director, Estelle Frankel, writes: "Our internal GPS, rooted in the innermost recesses of the soul, will guide us to our destination so long as we remain steadfast in our determination" (p. 16).

All great projects and inventions begin with this intensive pursuit of a dream, like Marcus Garvey's dream for Black people or Martin Luther King Jr.'s for an equitable society. Following these footpaths, Pope Francis' clarion call to synod is a call to dream. In *Let Us Dream*, he writes: "What I hear at this moment is similar to what Isaiah hears God saying through him: Come, let us talk this over. Let us dare to dream" (p. 6).

For Pope Francis, dreaming is a way of thinking that is open to the possibility of the Holy Spirit offering the Church something new. But to dream of a different future, he insists, "we need to choose fraternity over individualism as the organizing principle" (*Dream* p. 68).

The journey into the unknown that the biblical figures, Abraham and Sarah, were called on is an archetype of the Church's synod journey. Both heard a voice to embark upon a journey to an unknown and unnamed land. It was a call to leave the familiar – homeland, families, culture, habits – for the unfamiliar. Frankel identifies some key characteristics of their journey (pp. 26-29):

- They must **embark on the journey with faith** because the land to which they are called is uncharted territory. It is not a linear or straightforward journey; it is filled with twists and turns.

- When they stepped out into the unknown, their lives were **transformed** in all kinds of unanticipated ways. For example, angels disguised as men visited Abraham and Sarah unexpectedly and prophesied that Sarah would give birth to a son (Genesis 18:1-15).

- This unknown journey required the sacred use of imagination: "the ability to see things that are not yet visible or manifest." Abraham and Sarah's exercise of sacred imagination was shown in their hospitality to the strangers, who would pave the way for Abraham's later discovery that his descendants would number as many as the stars.

On this unknown synod journey, there is a choice to partner either with fear or faith. Fear stifles the imagination; it argues, "Well, we have had previous synods in my diocese and nothing has come out of them. I am not hopeful."

It was Pope St. John XXIII's sacred imagination that inspired him to convene the Second Vatican Council and withstand opposition, saying, "We feel we must disagree with those prophets of gloom, who are always forecasting disaster, as though the end of the world were at hand" (*Evangelii* #84). Prophets of gloom partner with fear; those who dream partner with faith.

As the Church embarks on this synodal journey into the unknown, we seek inspiration from countless biblical figures who did the same. Like them, we travel with faith as our inner companion. Faith allows the Holy Spirit to activate our sacred imagination and respond creatively like Abraham and Sarah. Faith will inspire us, the Church, to exercise our sacred imagination when we encounter the unknown.

And since it is an unknown journey of faith, the synodal journey can be described as a pilgrimage guided by spirituality. Sr. Nathalie Becquart, undersecretary for the Synod of Bishops, says of it:

> We must be precise, when we speak of synodality, of synodal journey, of synodal experience. It is not a parliament ... Synodality is not only the discussion of problems, of different things that there are in society ... There cannot be synodality without the Spirit, and there is no Spirit without prayer. (Patrignani)

Every participant must begin this journey with the intention of respectful dialogue, not imposing personal ideology, persuading other participants, or shouting down opposing views. It is in this spirit of dialogue and openness that the movement of the Holy Spirit reveals the secret destination of the Church.

Individual or Group Reflection

MISSIONARY CHALLENGE

As the Church embarks on this unknown synodal journey, we seek inspiration from countless biblical figures who did the same. Like them, we travel with faith as our inner companion. Faith allows the Holy Spirit to activate our sacred imagination and respond creatively like Abraham and Sarah. Faith will inspire us, the Church, to exercise our sacred imagination when we encounter the unknown.

SYNODAL EXERCISE

1. What is your biggest fear as you engage this synodal journey?
2. What support is required to transform your fear to faith?
3. Spend a few moments reflecting on this scripture passage:

    "Be anxious for nothing, but in everything by prayer and supplication, with thanksgiving, let your requests be made known to God; and the peace of God, which surpasses all understanding, will guard your hearts and minds through Christ Jesus" (Philippians 4:6-7).

    What is emerging for you?

CHAPTER SEVEN

Synod and Preparation

In the post-Vatican II Church, many dioceses conducted synods consisting of elected delegates from the laity, religious, and clergy. These assemblies were characterised by lengthy discussions and debates, movement of motions, and drafting of and voting on resolutions on priority areas for implementation.

In the Synod on Synodality, Pope Francis called for a three-year process that began in local dioceses on October 17, 2021, segued to the regional level, then to the universal Church in October 2023. What is the difference between this process and that of the synods referred to earlier?

Pope Francis understands the synod as a journey in which the People of God walk together to listen to each other and the Holy Spirit. In the previous chapter, I used the journeys of Abraham and Sarah (Genesis 18:1-15) as an archetype of the synodal journey. I have cited the Council of Jerusalem (Acts 15) as an example of the synodal process. Austen Ivereigh, the papal biographer, is insightful when he says:

> We'll all be on a crash course in synodality from November [2021]. [The synodal process is] firstly a process of discernment in a missionary key: its purpose is to invite the Holy Spirit to show the Church how we can better serve the world and evangelise ... Second, it's consultative, not deliberative: that is, it is designed to assist the bishops and ultimately the Pope ... Third, it is a process of mutual listening whose fruit, hopefully, is greater unity and shared purpose. (Dodd)

This premise assumes that participants know how to listen, are willing to do so, and are open to discovering something new on the journey. Realistically, we know that some participants bring their own predetermined agendas. Others come with ulterior motives, insecurities, fears, an accusatory finger, and mistrust. And still others listen only to what they wish to hear, numb to anything contrary to their opinions.

If the synod journey is to bear the anticipated fruits, participants must be honest and aware that we bring to this journey what Carl Jung calls our "shadow", that part of us that is so deeply unconscious that we experience it as a stranger to us. Jung posits that our first encounter with the shadow is in the form of projection – that which we reject in ourselves and identify in others.

In the narrative of the two disciples on the road to Emmaus (Luke 24:13-35), we witness the shadow in their response to Jesus' question. He asks, "What are you talking about as you walk along?" They respond: "You must be the only person in Jerusalem who does not know about the recent events." They're accusing Him of ignorance, essentially, projecting their own ignorance unto the Risen Christ.

How, then, can the synod journey move fruitfully ahead with our shadows? Jung writes: "One does not become enlightened by imagining figures of light, but by making the darkness conscious" (*Alchemical*, pp. 265-266). Jung advises awareness of our own shadows and the consequences of those shadows, and the integration of our shadows into our lives. There is a popular saying that goes: "That which we deny has control over us, but that which we confess, we have control over it." It is the awareness of our shadows that is key to a disposition of non-judgmental listening.

Jung would say that our "shadows" are not all that bad, it is our unconsciousness of them that is dangerous. Regarding the integration of our shadows, Estelle Frankel writes in *The Wisdom of Not Knowing*:

> It can also be a powerful source of energy and creativity. Once integrated, the shadow enables us to become whole. It is only destructive when it remains unconscious and compensates for an extremely unbalanced conscious attitude. (p. 68)

The disciples on the way to Emmaus are enlightened on their ignorance, or shadow, towards the end of their conversation with Jesus. It is this enlightenment, not the sterilisation of their shadow, that inspires them to exercise hospitality towards Jesus and return to Jerusalem. They were able to integrate, not purge, their own shadow. Of the fruit of this integration, Frankel says: "We become more tolerant of ourselves and others. We can more readily approach and make peace with our enemies because we no longer see them as our opposites, as completely 'other'" (p. 70).

The synodal journey, therefore, is not an event. It is an attitude and a spiritual disposition that opens us to authentic listening and dialogue. It is already occurring on social media, such as WhatsApp and Messenger, in parishes, offices, families, neighbourhoods, and dispute resolution sessions. We now face the current challenge of translating these synod-type journeys to the three-year synod of the Church.

Individual or Group Reflection

MISSIONARY CHALLENGE

The synodal journey, therefore, is not an event. It is an attitude and a spiritual disposition that opens us to authentic listening and dialogue.

SYNODAL EXERCISE

Prayer:

Lord, reveal my shadows to me. Create in me a desire for authentic listening during dialogue. Show me the way.

Spend ten minutes in silence, just being in the presence of the Holy Spirit, and listening.

CHAPTER EIGHT

The Aged

We have a natural attraction to youth: toddlers' plump cheeks, children's silky-smooth skin, the exuberant light-heartedness of adolescence. The sculpted bodies of athletes or the luxuriant hair that favours young men and women.

We find a plethora of such images splayed across fashion magazine pages, occupying major movie storylines and romantic song lyrics, invaluable tools for boosting traffic on social media platforms. Many persons, consciously and unconsciously, may yet find themselves singing the line, "Forever young, I want to be forever young", from Alphaville's 1984 hit song, *Forever Young*.

On the flip side of the coin of life, the aged experience no such attention. It seems flabby muscles, wrinkles, bodily frailty, grey hair or baldness, and limited, swift-as-snail movements thrusts them to the margins of desirability. Largely invisible in movies, magazines, and musical lyrics, their fame and lifetime achievements are often forgotten until their deaths. They are considered bothersome, hidden away in nursing homes, and in far too many cases, infrequently visited.

Pope Francis has made statements countering ageism. In an August 2022 papal audience, he said: "Old age ... is where wisdom is woven, which in turn illuminates the lives of younger generations and the entire community" (Watkins).

Archbishop Emeritus Edgerton Clarke of the Archdiocese of Kingston, Jamaica, shares a similar pastoral perspective. Now well into his nineties, he says that persons who are incapacitated, such as the aged, deeply need the human touch of a visit, a telephone call, a physical touch, or a listening ear. He insists that every priest prioritise and structure time in his busy life to spend with them. Pope Francis agrees, saying at the audience:

> In our old age, the importance of the many 'details' of which life is made – a caress, a smile, a gesture, an appreciated effort, an unexpected surprise, a hospitable cheerfulness, a faithful bond – becomes more acute. (Watkins)

For this reason, the Synod 2021-2024 logo includes youth alongside aged and wheelchair-bound persons. It's a clear-cut aide-mémoire that the aged accompanies the Church on the synodal journey with their wisdom, and the Church accompanies them with physical strength and a thirst for their wisdom.

Individual or Group Reflection

MISSIONARY CHALLENGE

It's a clear-cut aide-mémoire that the aged accompanies the Church on the synodal journey with their wisdom, and the Church accompanies them with physical strength and a thirst for their wisdom.

SYNODAL EXERCISE

1. At which end of the spectrum are you? Are you incapacitated in the wheelchair, the aged brimming with wisdom? Or are you one who accompanies with physical strength and a genuine thirst for the wisdom of the elderly?
2. What does it mean to accompany someone with your physical strength and a thirst for their wisdom?
3. How is God speaking to us in this moment?

CHAPTER NINE

Ecclesial Bunkers

Within community life, we have been injured by the bullets of persons' tongues, writings, or inaction. Perhaps a parish priest failed to visit during an illness, or parishioners were inhospitable at Mass. Gossiping tongues may have exposed my inner world, while hierarchical infighting plots against upward mobility.

When we are emotionally injured, the human tendency is often to declare war to protect ourselves from dreaded occurrences. We construct emotional bunkers, encircle ourselves with social barbed-wire fences, acquire the lethal weapon of silent treatment. We may aggressively recruit an army of supporters and launch verbal attacks on our enemies from our bunkers. Warfare is the response to our traumas.

"As fear hardens," Brown explains in *Braving the Wilderness*, "it expands and becomes less of a protective barrier and more of a solidifying division. It forces its way down in the gaps and tears apart our social foundation..." (p. 52).

On the synodal journey, the People of God face ecclesial bunkers: bishops against bishops, priests against bishops, priests against priests, parishioners against priests, conservative Catholics against liberal Catholics. The result of groups hiding in and attacking from their respective bunkers is a Church unable to effectively exercise its missionary mandate. Remember: "Every city or house divided against itself shall not stand" (Matthew 12:25).

Is there a way to build bridges of reconnection? The answer lies in the words of Christianna Paul, a youth of the Diocese of Roseau, Commonwealth of Dominica. She was sharing her experience of the synodal journey during the Antilles Episcopal Conference Annual Plenary Meeting held via Zoom in 2022. Paul said:

> I feel like there was more that could have been said, and so, I think this should be a continuous journey. ... It's not a duty we're fulfilling. [We] were building a relationship, ... so I hope that the consultations, ... and those safe spaces for people to talk about relevant topics, continue....

This is a clarion call for a brave and courageous willingness to be vulnerable, to exit our bunkers with a peace flag. A call to begin engaging in those tough, uncomfortable conversations with our perceived enemies. As long as we remain in our bunkers, says Brown, we die of loneliness and disconnection (p. 54). On this synodal journey, how can we emerge from the bunkers of Church life?

Individual or Group Reflection

MISSIONARY CHALLENGE

This is a clarion call for a brave and courageous willingness to be vulnerable, to exit our bunkers with a peace flag. A call to begin engaging in those tough, uncomfortable conversations with our perceived enemies. As long as we remain in our bunkers, we die of loneliness and disconnection.

SYNODAL EXERCISE

1. What is one issue in your personal and/or Church life that you are reluctant to openly discuss owing to fear of repercussions or other consequences?
2. If the space were created for you to speak, what might you say about the issue?
3. God knows your thoughts and needs even before they are expressed. Pause and hear what His response might be. Read and ponder Hebrews 4:12.

CHAPTER TEN

Walking Together

Synod is walking together,
Not running.
Running is speed.
Speed is end focussed: who will arrive first?
Arrival is victory.
Victory is reward,
Not for the group, but for one.

Synod is walking together,
Not running.
Walking is slowness.
Slowness is awareness,
Awareness of the other.
Awareness of the other is attention.
Attention is concern,

WALKING TOGETHER

Concern for the other.
Concern is care.
Care is compassion and mercy.
Compassion and mercy is stopping,
Stopping for the other.
Stopping is not future focussed,
It's present.

Synod is walking together,
Not running.
Synod is intercourse:
Inter (Latin): "between" + *currere* (Latin): "run".
Synod is feeling the Spirit that draws us together.
Synod is courting the other.
Synod is inviting the other.
It's slow.
It's deliberate.
It's mindful intercourse.

Synod is arousal
Of emotions, thoughts, and inspiration.
Synod is messy.
Synod is care.
It's compassion.

Synod is intercourse.
Intercourse gives birth,

WALKING TOGETHER

Birth to new life.
New life, new gifts,
New world.
Synod is walking together.

Individual or Group Reflection

MISSIONARY CHALLENGE

Synod is walking together,
Not running.
Walking is slowness.
Slowness is awareness,
Awareness of the other.

SYNODAL EXERCISE

1. In Chapter 1, we began to listen more attentively. How might "running" and "busy-ness" impact the quality of your listening?
2. Reflect on what happens when you slow down or pause at a traffic light. What do you become more aware of in yourself and in others?
3. Where do you experience God's presence?

CHAPTER ELEVEN

Home Garden: Imperfect Icon of Synodality

The magnificent beauty of the garden rests in the diversity of birds, insects, reptiles, and plants – their various colours, sizes, and types. The diversity, we might say, of participants in communion, in symbiotic relationship. Individually, each element would lack beauty, function, and purpose, but these diverse members are like companions on a journey. And on that journey, there is togetherness, coexistence.

The garden companions on this journey are on a mission to gift earth with oxygen and purify it of carbon dioxide. A mission to provide food, beauty, and rest, respite for passing parrots going to and from work. They can also be ascribed theatrical roles:

- The **Protagonist** would be the sun, the source of light and life. Every member resurrects at its appearance. It is like a magnet, for the leaves follow its direction.

- The **Crowd** is represented by the diversity of plants, birds, insects, and reptiles who traverse the garden or make their home in it.
- The **Apostles** would be my banana plants and Christmas palms, present in the garden from the beginning. The palms' height and age exude leadership and wisdom.
- And the fourth actor on stage: The **Antagonist**, represented by the bachacs (very large ants) and mealybugs. The antagonist's mission is to destroy and disrupt the symbiotic relationship.

The garden respects silence; silent listening. Listening to the needs of the birds, iguanas, and humans for food and peace, for comfort, shade, and rest. There's conversion, and a conversation between the guava and banana trees. Planted beside each other, they negotiate the use of the tiny space. In competition, at first; then in co-operation, learning to coexist in a confined space.

Synod: companions on a journey.

My home garden: an imperfect icon of the Synod.

Those who have eyes to see, let them see the Church journeying together through the imperfect lens of my home garden.

Individual or Group Reflection

MISSIONARY CHALLENGE

Individually, each element would lack beauty, function, and purpose, but these diverse members are like companions on a journey. And on that journey, there is togetherness, coexistence.

SYNODAL EXERCISE

1. What emotions surface in you when you consider a journey of togetherness and coexistence?
2. Is there any hint of resistance? If so, what does it stem from?
3. How might you experience God's presence in the togetherness?

CHAPTER TWELVE

Synodal Waves

Synodality:
   A community in dialogue
   leading to discernment,
   decision-making, decision-taking,
   implementing, evaluating.

To what can I liken this way of living as a Church?
Like a sea crab, I bury my butt on a sandy beach,
Facing rolling waves crashing a short distance from
   my feet.
Closing my eyes, focussing on the sounds,
Then opening them to marry the sound
To the sight of the waves.

WALKING TOGETHER

My eyes capture distant white waves,
noticing their dynamic
ebb and flow,
rising and dying,
until depositing sand on the shore to form the beach.

Synodal waves:
    The ongoing ebb and flow
    of dialogue, discernment,
    decision-making,
    implementation, evaluation.
    Each action feeding the other,
    building in momentum,
    and finally,
    accomplishing their mission –
    the beach.

But synodal waves also deconstruct beaches,
    changing, reshaping the mission.
This is a time of deconstruction,
    reshaping our modus operandi and modus vivendi
    for more effective mission.

Synodal waves act not on their own,
    but are guided and directed
    by the Spirit Wind,
    a powerful invisible Source.

"When the Advocate comes, whom I will send to you from the Father, He will testify about Me" (John 15:26).

In common, synodal waves
- cooperate with the Wind,
- open to the Wind,
- listen to the Wind,
- surrender to the Wind.

This is a synodal time.

Let's ride the synodal waves to carry us forward on mission.

Individual or Group Reflection

MISSIONARY CHALLENGE

Synodal waves:
The ongoing ebb and flow
of dialogue, discernment,
decision-making,
implementation, evaluation.
Each action feeding the other,
building in momentum,
and finally,
accomplishing their mission –
the beach.

SYNODAL EXERCISE

1. What image might depict or represent your synodal journey as you consider building community with others, including the marginalised, and having dialogue with those whose voices are not usually heard?
2. Describe the key characteristics of the image and their significance to your journey.
3. How might you depict the presence of the Holy Spirit on this journey?

CHAPTER THIRTEEN

Synodality and Lent

How can the Lenten season enable the Church to become more synodal? During Lent, we retreat from the business of life to listen attentively to the voice of God calling us to repentance and conversion. The Church calls its members to deeper and more intense prayer, fasting, and almsgiving. While these are ongoing Christian activities, we are invited to focus and reflect on the season's spiritual value of self-sacrifice.

The gospel reading on Ash Wednesday, the first day of Lent, from Matthew 6:1-6, 16-21, speaks of the purpose of fasting, praying, and almsgiving. The desert is a commonly used metaphor in Scripture to describe a period in which individuals or communities lose the power of total control over their external life circumstances. They possess, however, the power to respond by managing and negotiating the space. This desert phase triggers feelings of helplessness and weakness. It tames the ego, causing us to stare at the stark reality of our own dispensability, finitude, and limitations.

Since there aren't any deserts in the Caribbean, perhaps a more suitable metaphor would be hurricanes, where the only power we have is simply to prepare to wait out the storm. This phase of powerlessness is often described as liminal, originating from the Latin word *limen*, meaning "threshold" – a point or place of entering or beginning.

A liminal space is the time between the "what was" and the "next" – a place of transition, of waiting, of not knowing. It is an opportunity for transformation. Richard Rohr says we have to allow ourselves to be drawn out of "business as usual" and remain patiently on the "threshold", for:

> It's the realm where God can best get at us because our false certitudes are finally out of the way. This is the sacred space where the old world is able to fall apart, and a bigger world is revealed. (*Everything,* pp. 155-156)

The season of Lent is an unforced invitation into liminal space, but real-life circumstances can force individuals into it. Recent happenings in the universal Church have forced us into this liminal space. These include the loss of our moral and authoritative voice on global and moral issues owing to our mismanagement of the sex abuse issue. The upsurge of competing religious and secular voices of authority, the loss of respectability in some societies and of political power and control, along with the declining rate of Catholic populations have also propelled us into this liminal space. The Roman collar and religious garb no longer gain us automatic respect and trust. In some respects, the Church is grieving the loss of power, control, and influence. How must the Church respond? Where the synodal process coincides with the season of Lent, the People of God are invited to journey together into this "post-hurricane", liminal space.

The hurricanes of local and global forces have stripped us bare. The coronavirus pandemic threw us into a space of the unknown, unable to immediately provide prepared theological and spiritual answers for the questions emerging from this Volatile, Uncertain, Complex, Ambiguous (VUCA) period. Now we must learn to abandon dependence on and addiction to the silo of authoritative voices of pastoral leaders and learn to trust the *sensus fidelium,* the voice of the People of God, through a process of listening, guided by the word of God and prayer.

The consultative period of the synodal journey, guided by a certain spirituality, attitude, and the questionnaires, understandably triggers feelings of discomfort and awkwardness in the Church. The journey will be imperfect. Mistakes will be made. It will be messy. It is to be expected; these are the characteristics of the liminal phase.

Remaining faithful to the roadmap given in the synodal handbook is crucial for the between and betwixt periods. It guides the Church through the valley of the shadow of death to the green pastures of a new way of being Church – a synodal Church.

Individual or Group Reflection

MISSIONARY CHALLENGE

The consultative period of the synodal journey, guided by a certain spirituality, attitude, and the questionnaires, understandably triggers feelings of discomfort and awkwardness in the Church. The journey will be imperfect. Mistakes will be made. It will be messy. It is to be expected; these are the characteristics of the liminal phase.

SYNODAL EXERCISE

1. What is your emotional response to a liminal space, the time between the "what was" and the "next", a place of transition, of waiting, and not knowing? Is it an opportunity for transformation? How do you manage yourself during uncertainty and the unknown?
2. What would help you in navigating this liminal space, this journey in which we will make mistakes?

Be anxious for nothing, but in everything by prayer and supplication, with thanksgiving, let your requests be made known to God; and the peace of God, which surpasses all understanding, will guard your hearts and minds through Christ Jesus. (Philippians 4:6-7)

CHAPTER FOURTEEN

Temptations as Pitfalls
(First Sunday of Lent, Year C - Luke 4:1-13)

Imagine you are a member of a group on a hiking trail. On the trail, you bump into huge rocks, running streams, fallen trees, and dangerous precipices. To navigate these dangerous obstacles, you need to be equipped with skills.

On the synodal journey, there are obstacles or temptations of which we should be aware. Today's gospel reading of Luke's account of the temptation of Jesus unveils two insights:

- The obstacles that Jesus faces on His missionary journey.
- Jesus' reliance on the Holy Spirit for heightened awareness and the power to resist evil.

Similarly, the synodal journey is a Spirit-driven one. The same Spirit that inspires and empowers Jesus equips the Church today to be aware of and resist the obstacles.

The temptation narrative presents three broad categories of temptations. These are:

- Unbridled reliance on self.
- Indispensable, exclusive power.
- Putting God to the test.

The synod handbook refers to these temptations as "pitfalls" (2.4) and lists nine which can be grouped under the categories above.

Category 1 – Unbridled reliance on self:

- Wanting to lead ourselves instead of being led by God.
- Focussing on ourselves and our immediate concerns.
- Seeing only "problems".

Category 2 – Indispensable, exclusive power:

- Focussing only on structures.
- Not looking beyond the visible confines of the Church.
- Losing focus of the objectives of the synodal process.

Category 3 – Putting God to the test:

- Treating the synod as a parliament.
- Conflict and division.
- Listening only to those who are already involved in Church.

TEMPTATIONS AS PITFALLS

Pitfalls, or temptations, the inclination to not rely on God, is part and parcel of the Church's synodal journey. Luke's temptation narrative reminds the Church to rely on the Holy Spirit to navigate the Lenten synodal journey. I invite you to carefully reflect on your personal and communal experience of any of these pitfalls.

Individual or Group Reflection

MISSIONARY CHALLENGE

Pitfalls, or temptations, the inclination to not rely on God, is part and parcel of the Church's synodal journey. Luke's temptation narrative reminds the Church to rely on the Holy Spirit to navigate the Lenten synodal journey.

SYNODAL EXERCISE

Recall an experience when you unwittingly or unintentionally placed God on the back burner.
1. What were the highs and lows of this experience?
2. Did you eventually replace God up front and centre?
3. What are your learnings from this experience?

CHAPTER FIFTEEN

Transfiguration Moments
(Second Sunday of Lent, Year C - Luke 9:28-36)

The Gospel of Luke (Year C) is an ideal synodal gift to the Church because Luke crafts Jesus' ministry as a journey, beginning on the plains of Galilee and upwards to Jerusalem with His disciples. Guided by the Holy Spirit, Jesus forms missionary disciples on that journey.

In today's gospel, there is a transfiguration moment along the way. In a mountaintop experience, as Moses had on Sinai, three of the disciples, Peter, James, and John, experience a theophany in Jesus – a visible manifestation of God. In this encounter, a voice from the cloud declares of Jesus: "This is My Son, the Chosen One. Listen to Him." The voice confirms and reassures the disciples that Jesus is, without doubt, truly divine and the Chosen One.

The start of the journey had been turbulent and challenging, so the disciples really needed this mountaintop encounter as spiritual and psychological fuel for the remainder of their travels. Jesus' journey to Jerusalem is a model for the synodal journey. There are challenging, despairing, disheartening, confusing, and perplexing times – moments of desolation. These, however, are punctuated with "mountaintop" experiences, moments of consolation where we encounter God's intimate presence. In these encounters, we are reminded to listen to Jesus.

For this reason, the synod handbook, the *Vademecum*, says that the synodal journey is the People of God walking together, "listening to the Holy Spirit and the Word of God..." (1.2). These "mountaintop" encounters bring us to conversion, that is, resisting the temptation to be fixated in our way of thinking and acting, as illustrated by Peter's tent-building suggestion. They also serve to refresh and encourage us to keep moving on together to Jerusalem, where we will experience crucifixion of the self, resurrection to new life, and an outpouring of the Holy Spirit for mission.

How have you been transformed by transfiguration moments? How has your community been transformed by its transfiguration moments?

Individual or Group Reflection

MISSIONARY CHALLENGE

These "mountaintop" encounters bring us to conversion, that is, resisting the temptation to be fixated in our way of thinking and acting, as illustrated by Peter's tent-building suggestion. They also serve to refresh and encourage us to keep moving on together to Jerusalem, where we will experience crucifixion of the self, resurrection to new life, and an outpouring of the Holy Spirit for mission.

SYNODAL EXERCISE

1. Have you found a community with which you can undertake a synodal journey?
2. How have you or how has your community been transformed by transfiguration moments?
3. Where is the Holy Spirit leading you?

CHAPTER SIXTEEN

Priestly Anniversary Gift

Prior to her birth
Bonnie kicked up a storm
In the womb of the Caribbean Sea,
Creating mayhem on the day
Of my priestly anniversary.

Before the sun rose and changed her pyjamas,
My eyes opened.
I lay in silent darkness,
With slight disturbances from streetlights
Fighting to penetrate
The room's natural darkness.

WALKING TOGETHER

My mind gave birth to an ordination memory:
Lying face down in cruciform position,
Prostrate on the Cathedral floor
As Grace – the sun – awoke.
She arose in radiant beauty,
Adorned in her "Sunday best".

Ready to boast to the neighbours,
She exited her house beyond the mountains,
Sailed majestically down the street in glory.
But some dark storm-cloud neighbours
Threatened to dampen her spirit.

Cheers of hooray
Bellowed from my heart,
Because I needed her rays
As a gift to celebrate my anniversary.
I cheered and clapped
As her dazzling rays rose.
But the presence of storm-cloud neighbours
Counteracted with jeers of darkness.

Refusing to be daunted
Her rays fought back,
And touched the heart of a priest
To pay me a visit.

PRIESTLY ANNIVERSARY GIFT

Slowed to a crawl by Parkinson's,
Words of wisdom flowed from his heart:

"I must learn to gradually let go of my independence.
Synodality is journeying together.
Priest journeying with laity,
Laity journeying with priests.
I need to allow the people to journey with me
In my physical weakness."

With visit ended,
Jealous storm-cloud neighbours regrouped.
Spouting rain and thunderstorm.
Forcing postponement of Carnival-like celebrations.
Forcing the befriending of aloneness.

The space of aloneness
Propelled me back
Thirty years ago:
Prostrate and alone on the Cathedral floor,
Yet surrounded by the People of God.
Yep, my anniversary gift from Grace:
Aloneness…
Like a log floating in the vast ocean
Of the People of God.

(Written June 28, 2022,
the day of my 30th priestly anniversary)

Individual or Group Reflection

MISSIONARY CHALLENGE

Synodality is journeying together.
Priest journeying with laity,
Laity journeying with priests.
I need to allow the people to journey with me
In my physical weakness.

SYNODAL EXERCISE

Prayer:
Heavenly Father, open my mind and my heart that I may be transformed during this synodal journey. Grant me the humility necessary for me to be vulnerable, allowing others to journey with me in my weakness. Grant me compassion that I may listen attentively to others and act from the understanding of their experiences. I ask this in Jesus' name. Amen.

After reciting the prayer, spend five minutes in silence, discerning what the Holy Spirit may be laying on your heart.

CHAPTER SEVENTEEN

Building a Synodal Church

In building magnificent structures, such as bridges, skyscrapers, ocean liners, and bullet trains, human beings have learnt and applied some fundamental lessons. One such lesson is that development is a painstakingly slow process, devoid of shortcuts. Moreover, the journey towards completion entails challenges that, once embraced, stimulate creativity and innovation.

Throughout history, we have admired persons such as St. Teresa of Calcutta, St. Martin de Porres, Dr. Martin Luther King, and Nelson Mandela. Their lives are a testament to the Jamaican saying: "A swif mek wass-wass no gedder honey", which means, "It is because of haste that wasps don't gather honey". The lesson here is to be strategic in life, move deliberately and slowly. Don't be hasty. This approach to life is surely contrary to a contemporary culture characterised by individualism and the tendency to swiftly abandon ship when challenges arise.

Building a synodal Church is a slow growth process that requires the engine of stability. An "inner energy", says Joan Chittister, "that guides us up one hill after another in life" and gives us the "capacity for dealing with all the dimensions of life in an equitable and reasonable manner" (*The Monastic Heart*, pp. 158-159).

It was stability and perseverance that enabled enslaved Africans to resist the evil actions of European conquerors for four centuries. They envisioned not only their own freedom, but that of their children and their children's children.

To grow a synodal Church, we must dream of it and be active participants in the journey to fulfilling that dream. Our participation ought to involve preparing the soil of hearts and minds to listen, dialogue, and discern, planting the seeds of God's word and watering the soil with the wisdom of life lessons.

Participation also includes weeding out thinking and behavioural patterns that are contrary to Gospel values. It involves pruning dead, ideologically non-synodal branches, those that are solitary and resist engagement. It is a slow painstaking pilgrimage, requiring patience and perseverance, that gradually reveals the fruits of the synodal journey.

Individual or Group Reflection

MISSIONARY CHALLENGE

Our participation ought to involve preparing the soil of hearts and minds to listen, dialogue, and discern, planting the seeds of God's word and watering the soil with the wisdom of life lessons. Participation also includes weeding out thinking and behavioural patterns that are contrary to Gospel values. It involves pruning dead, ideologically non-synodal branches, those that are solitary or resist engagement.

SYNODAL EXERCISE

Meditation can be used to prepare the soil of our hearts and minds to listen, dialogue, and discern. What are some other spiritual practices that could assist you in watering and planting seed in the soil during this synodal journey?

CHAPTER EIGHTEEN

A Graced Journey

I have vivid memories of my first road trip to the Cumana Retreat House in Cumana, Trinidad and Tobago. Operated by the Sisters of St. Joseph of Cluny, I received clear instructions to locate it: "Pay keen attention to the concrete milestones along the roadway. The most important one is milestone number 33.5."

It was night when I drove along the winding, mountainous coastal roadway, my journey slow and deliberate. I kept an eye out for the various inconspicuous, often poorly maintained, milestone posts along the route. But finding the location was possible because the engineers who designed and built the road used these milestone posts as the principal guide for travellers. The synodal journey is like this.

> Synod is a journey.
> Not a lonesome journey,

WALKING TOGETHER

a communal journey:
"We are companions on a journey."

Synod is a journey.
Not individuals making singular decisions,
but communal listening, discerning, and deciding.

Synod is a journey.
A journey along an unknown route.
Though unknown, there's a route
travelled by ancestors of faith.

Synod is a journey.
A route.
A stony, rugged, winding, dirty, muddy,
ascending and descending route.

Synod is a journey.
The engineer of God's Spirit goes before us
to prepare the route with milestones.

Synod is a journey.
A journey inviting openness,
listening to the Spirit.
Listening to the community for instructions:
"Pay attention to the milestones."

Synod is a journey.
Littered with

ideological,
emotional,
religious,
socio-economic distractions.

Synod is a journey.
Now is the time to listen, dialogue, and discern,
Paying close attention to milestones,
the signs of the times.
Equipping community
with Scripture and Tradition.

He has risen from the dead and now he is going before you to Galilee; it is there you will see him. (Matthew 28:7)

Individual or Group Reflection

MISSIONARY CHALLENGE

Synod is a journey.
Now is the time to listen, dialogue, and discern,
Paying close attention to milestones,
the signs of the times.
Equipping community
with Scripture and Tradition.

SYNODAL EXERCISE

Read today's scripture. As you reflect on it in the context of current times, what milestones can you identify?

CHAPTER NINETEEN

Dialectic

A brief conversation between my Mom and Dad offered an insight into one aspect of synodality.

The gardener arrived at their home early one morning. Mom informed Dad that she was going to prepare breakfast for him. My father asked, "Do you really have to prepare breakfast for him?"

Later, Mom shared with me that she would normally prepare breakfast, and even dinner, for the gardener to take home. What's happening in this scenario?

My father's focus is on the goal, the destination. From his perspective, the gardener comes for the sole purpose of getting the job done. On the other hand, Mom's focus is on the journey – the <u>now</u>. In her mind, she seems to ask, "How is he going to arrive at the destination without fuel for the journey?" Her interest points to relationship-building, that is, paying attention to the human person along the journey.

Dad and Mom represent the dialectical tension of the entire journey – the <u>now</u>: the journey, and the <u>not yet</u>: the destination. Without a focus on the destination, we risk chasing our own tails. Without a focus on the journey and the relationships along the way, we risk achieving the measurable goal with broken, wounded relationships, or not achieving the goal at all.

There's another aspect of the synodal journey to consider. If the People of God are called to journey together to listen to each other and the Holy Spirit, then we need to be prepared to face a diversity of personality types, idiosyncrasies, perspectives, spiritualities, skill sets, and social and intellectual capacities. All of which we learn to hold in tension.

Synodality invites us to utilise our human and material resources to equip participants on the journey to dialogue, discern, decide, and implement.

Individual or Group Reflection

MISSIONARY CHALLENGE

If the People of God are called to journey together to listen to each other and the Holy Spirit, then we need to be prepared to face a diversity of personality types, idiosyncrasies, perspectives, spiritualities, skill sets, and social and intellectual capacities. All of which we learn to hold in tension.

SYNODAL EXERCISE

1. How might you be challenged by the diversity of persons you encounter on this synodal journey?
2. What diversity element, or area of difference, may you find most difficult to engage with? Personalities? Spiritualities? Intelligence or social class?
3. What can you do to manage the tensions that may arise?
4. How did Jesus manage tensions in diversity?

CHAPTER TWENTY

Human Family

The journey to building a synodal Church can seem like the ascent of a steep and rugged hill. Some years ago, four friends and I agreed to hike up a steep mountain. On the way to the starting point, I noticed a bottle of whiskey and a few glasses in the car. At the foot of the mountain, two of them suggested that the three stronger climbers go ahead and they would straggle behind.

On the ascent, there was no sign of the stragglers. We continued, notwithstanding, exhilarated by the adrenaline of the climb and the spectacular views at the summit and during the descent. At the base of the mountain, we were greeted by our two companions seated on a rock, drinking scotch on the rocks.

A synodal Church involves the People of God walking together on mission, listening to each other and the Holy Spirit in a process of discerning, deciding, implementing, and evaluating. The power of decision-making rests in the hands of the community.

The discerning and decision-making process is tedious, winding, and time-consuming, as opposed to the easier way of abdicating decision-making into the clenched fists of a few. The enemy of this communal and participatory way of decision-making is the whiskey of self-gratification that keeps our motives and interests at base level.

In *The Monastic Heart*, Joan Chittister reminds us that we are socialised to work for ourselves alone. Our money, status, and security are most important, rather than the quality of the community or society as a whole. It's easier to inebriate ourselves with the tired and worn-out paradigm of the few deciding for the many, enforcing decisions, and dragging the whole along (p. 115).

A synodal Church says, "No! As a team of hikers, we should have started and ended together. No one should be left behind. The weak and the strong travel together. The three should not leave the others behind at the start of the ascent."

Synodality invites conversion from self-gratification to communal gratification, thinking of the needs of the parish or family community, the societal and global community, and the human family.

The *Vademecum for the Synod on Synodality* – the synod's official handbook – reminds us: "We are all in the same boat. Together we form the Body of Christ. Setting aside the mirage of self-sufficiency, we are able to learn from each other, journey together, and be at the service of one another" (2.3).

Individual or Group Reflection

MISSIONARY CHALLENGE

The discerning and decision-making process is tedious, winding, and time-consuming, as opposed to the easier way of abdicating decision-making into the clenched fists of a few.

SYNODAL EXERCISE

1. What are the challenges you encounter when you have to accomplish a task alongside someone who may not be as fit or as knowledgeable as you?
2. What are the challenges you encounter when the roles are reversed, when you are the one with less knowledge or are less fit for the task?
3. What would help you stay alongside the other person?
4. How might you apply this wisdom on the synodal journey?
5. How might your journey with God inform what you choose to do?

CHAPTER TWENTY-ONE

Leadership

Pastoral leaders are formed and called to serve the community into which they are born. Historically, communities intentionally built the capacity of its members so that each became a leader in her or his own way and right.

The historically nomadic culture of the Israelite community, for example, was the environment that honed the pastoral leadership skills of David, the Hebrew king. His skills of pasturing sheep, passed down from generation to generation, were shaped from childhood. He learned to pasture in death-defying valleys and other perilous physical environments. He slept with the sheep at nights, risking his personal safety to search for them when lost, protect them from fierce wolves, and daily lead them to green pastures. Through his life as a shepherd, David learnt to face fear of the enemy.

After the parents of twelve-year-old Jesus located Him in the Temple at Jerusalem, He obediently returned with them to Nazareth. Luke's gospel says of Him: "And Jesus grew in wisdom and stature, and in favour with God and man" (Luke 2:52). Like His ancestor, David, Jesus' pastoral leadership was fashioned in the cultural, historical, and religious texture of the Jewish community.

According to the International Theological Commission, synodality is "a process of decision-making through a joint exercise of discernment, consultation, and co-operation" (Synodality #69). Pastoral leaders who are decision-makers are called, therefore, to live in the Spirit. They must learn to discern the movement of, and co-operate with, the Spirit in community. Personal discernment of the Spirit is the fundamental service Servant leaders offer to communities.

The priestly ministry issues from among the baptised. Priests are formed in and by the community to lead it in collective listening and discernment. The priestly ministry is not an election to a privileged status, but a communally discerned call to the service of listening and discernment. Emerging from the raw and messy priesthood of the faithful, the priest presides over the community by acting *in persona Christi*. Consequently, the priest is formed with the consciousness that the Word of God has been entrusted to the "entire holy people united with their shepherds" (*Dei Verbum* # 10), and together, "form one single consensus"; in Latin: *fidelium conspiratio* (Luciani, p. 37).

If the community called the Church needs priests with the heart of Jesus, the Good Shepherd, capable of listening, discerning, making and taking decisions together with the People of God, then the formation of their leadership and pastoral capacities begin and continue within the community called the Church.

Individual or Group Reflection

MISSIONARY CHALLENGE

Priests are formed in and by the community to lead it in collective listening and discernment. The priestly ministry is not an election to a privileged status, but a communally discerned call to the service of listening and discernment.

SYNODAL EXERCISE

1. How can I support priestly ministry during this synodal journey?
2. What is God asking of me?

CHAPTER TWENTY-TWO

Synodality and Catechesis

The spirit and guidelines of the synodal journey are, without doubt, gifts to all, particularly to catechists – these are formators, teachers of the faith. In this chapter, we explore the image of catechesis – this is religious instruction, teaching of the faith – as being at two ends of a seesaw.

At one end, there is catechesis as defined in Pope St. John Paul II's 1979 apostolic exhortation, *Catechesi Tradendae*: "[A]n education in the faith of children, young people, and adults..." (#18). Faith, a gift or spark from God given at baptism, is fanned into flame (1 Timothy 1:6) by an ongoing organic and systematic pedagogy, or teaching method, called catechesis. If we are born with innumerable potentials, we need a formal and informal education system to unearth those potentials.

Catechesis, therefore, embraces the Church's faith in the mystery of God and passes it on in a contemporary and relevant package. The elements passed on encompass all that is revealed in the Person and mission of Jesus Christ (Scriptures) and the Church's practice through the centuries (Tradition). This is a lived faith, demonstrated by countless witnesses throughout the centuries as they negotiated religious persecution, social injustices, suffering, and socio-economic hardships.

At the other end of our seesaw, we have the current synodal journey and the handbook that serves as a roadmap for the People of God. Together, the people listen to each other and the Holy Spirit as they discern what the Holy Spirit is saying to the Church today. On this faith journey, discernment consists of everyone boldly speaking and attentively listening to each other's raw faith experiences.

At the fulcrum, or pivotal point, between catechesis and the synodal journey are the catechists: persons formally and informally trained, tasked with passing on the faith. In the ministry of faith formation, they play a central role in developing the unique relationship between teaching of the faith and the synod journey. To help catechists further understand their pivotal role, I use the narrative of the Emmaus disciples as a model of faith formation (Luke 24:13-35).

Catechists take the initiative and insert themselves in the centre of the raw and messy lives of the people, as Jesus did with the distraught, confused, and fed-up disciples. Parents, clergy, and faith formators spend time during formation to enquire, "What's happening?"; "How are you feeling?"; "What are your thoughts?"

Questions such as these create safe, secure, and trustworthy spaces for the participants to speak freely and courageously about their life experiences and how they perceive these in relation to their faith. Catechists may need to gently persist in asking these questions since participants may not speak immediately. Some may be fearful, lacking trust and/or confidence.

Catechists listen attentively, and non-judgmentally, to participants' stories of sadness and joy, failure and success, despair and hope, frustration and satisfaction. They resist the temptation to analyse, simply receiving what is being spoken, as Jesus did with the Emmaus disciples.

Having listened deeply with the "ear of the heart" (Francis, *Listening*), catechists can now relate the participants' stories to the richness of our Christian faith, as revealed in the Scriptures and the Church's Tradition. It is essential that catechists be familiar with the wealth of the Bible and the Church's Tradition in order to draw easily from these. This knowledge, and its wise application, can help participants discern the presence of the Holy Spirit in their current life circumstances.

The Emmaus model also demonstrates the importance of community and hospitality in faith formation. Catechesis is a ministry that is executed in the context of community. At the outset of His ministry, Jesus chooses the Twelve to live in communion with Him (Mark 3:14). The *Aparecida* document says: "Faith releases us from the isolation of the 'Me', because it leads us to communion" (#156).

It is in communion that participants discover solidarity. They learn that the faith Tradition offers meaning for their current circumstances. In Luke's narrative, the Risen Jesus stays with the disciples and celebrates a "meal", at the end of which they proclaim, "Did not our hearts burn within us?"

We see that the catechetical approach of the Risen Lord was not primarily about teaching doctrine or preparing the disciples for the sacraments, but about journeying with them, helping them to grow in faith in preparation for mission. That growth in faith consists of conversion, changing from seeing with the eyes of their emotions and thoughts to seeing with the eyes of faith in preparation for mission. Essentially, changing the direction of their lives.

Catechists have the awesome responsibility of preparing children, young people, and adults for **mission,** journeying with them through **communion** and **participation**. To do this, they must have intimate knowledge of the synodal journey and have experienced their own personal conversion. This synodal journey and its handbook, therefore, are invaluable gifts to all, and in particular, to catechists.

Individual or Group Reflection

MISSIONARY CHALLENGE

Catechists have the awesome responsibility of preparing children, young people, and adults for **mission,** journeying with them through **communion** and **participation**. To do this, they must have intimate knowledge of the synodal journey and have experienced their own personal conversion.

SYNODAL EXERCISE

1. What has been your personal experience of sacramental formation?
2. Did you experience:
    i. Being accompanied on your journey?
    ii. Growth in your knowledge of doctrine?
    iii. Growth in faith?
    iv. Personal conversion?
    v. A readiness for mission?
3. What worked well? What did not work so well?
4. What is the Holy Spirit asking of you now?

CHAPTER TWENTY-THREE

Synodality and Conversations

The 2021-2024 Synod on Synodality focusses on the community of the baptised as they participate in a process of speaking and listening to discern the movement of the Holy Spirit in the mission of the Church. The synod's theme, "For a Synodal Church: Communion, Participation, and Mission", aptly captures the fundamental reason for this journey.

The synod journey comprises three phases: diocesan, regional, and universal. Pope Francis has invited all parishes, small Christian communities, lay movements, religious communities, and other forms of communion to participate. The gesture illustrates the synod's inherent inclusivity.

The office with responsibility for organising the synod has published a road map, the official handbook called the *Vademecum*, to guide the Church on this journey. According to the handbook, participation is characterised by the interrelated actions of speaking and listening. In a word, by conversation.

To shed light on the quality of conversation of which Pope Francis dreams, I will utilise insights on Conversational Intelligence→ (C-IQ). According to the CreatingWE Institute, a US-based executive coaching company:

> Conversational Intelligence→ is the intelligence hardwired into every human being to enable us to navigate successfully with others. Through language and conversations, we learn to build trust, to bond, to grow, and build partnerships with each other to create and transform our societies. (*Conversational*)

There are three levels of conversation. Level I is called "transactional conversation". This level of conversation is I-centred; participants simply exchange information to validate and confirm what they know.

Level II conversation is called "positional conversation", characterised by an exchange of power. Those engaged in this type of conversation defend what they know or attempt to influence and persuade others to agree with their point of view. It is an opportunity to seek a win-win solution.

Level III conversation is called "transformational conversation", involving exchange of energy. At this level, participants aim to discover what they do not know. It is a "Share-Discover" dynamic, a WE-centred conversation. Life coach, Evan Bernache, says people engaged in this level of conversation see things this way: "We hold the space to explore unchartered territory, we ask questions for which we have no answer" (Bernache).

Pope Francis desires that the Church participate in the synod journey utilising the mindset of Level III conversations. The handbook states that:

> Fostering participation leads us out of ourselves to involve others who hold different views than we do. Listening to those who have the same views as we do bears no fruit. Dialogue involves coming together across diverse opinions. ... We must make a special effort to listen to those we may be tempted to see as unimportant and those who force us to consider new points of view that may change our way of thinking. (2.2)

It is an invitation to enter the process with a WE-centred mindset, thinking of the common good, not individual pursuit through debate, arguing, or lobbying. To participate meaningfully in a Level III conversation surely requires mutual trust. The handbook states:

> It is especially important that this listening process happen in a spiritual setting that supports openness in sharing as well as hearing. ... In this way, our journey of listening to one another can be an authentic experience of discerning the voice of the Holy Spirit. Authentic discernment is made possible where there is time for deep reflection and a spirit of mutual trust, common faith, and a shared purpose. (1.1)

The handbook invites us to leave behind prejudices and stereotypes and cure the virus of self-sufficiency and ideologies (2.3). I believe Pope Francis dreams of participants becoming co-creators (Bernache). Co-creators have the mindset of building new meaning. Their inner disposition asks: "How can we create new possibilities together?" Their outer actions demonstrate a willingness to transform reality with others.

The characteristics of co-creators correspond closely to some attitudes that the synod committee desires for participants on the synod journey. These are humility in listening, courage in speaking, willingness to change our opinions based on what we have heard, conversion and change. Change is manifested when we abandon attitudes of complacency and comfort that can lead us to make decisions based purely on how things have been done in the past (*Vademecum* 2.3).

When local dioceses began their first synod stage, seeking "a broad consultation process in order to gather the wealth of the experiences of lived synodality" (*Preparatory* #31), I invited my blog readership to reflect on scripture passages that demonstrated synodality in action. I invite you to read and ponder the same: Acts 15:1-21 on the Council of Jerusalem, and these accounts of the miracle of the loaves: Matthew 14:13-21, Mark 6:30-44, Luke 9:10-17, and John 6:30-44.

Individual or Group Reflection

MISSIONARY CHALLENGE

The characteristics of co-creators correspond closely to some attitudes that the synod committee desires for participants on the synod journey. These are humility in listening, courage in speaking, willingness to change our opinions based on what we have heard, conversion and change. Change is manifested when we abandon attitudes of complacency and comfort that can lead us to make decisions based purely on how things have been done in the past.

SYNODAL EXERCISE

1. This synod journey calls us to be counterintuitive and countercultural, being and doing things that are not the norm. What are the emotions surfacing in you as you consider the changes required in your mind and heart?
2. What can you do to develop the patience, persistence, and resilience required for this journey?
3. How might your community support you on this journey?

Scripture Reflection

"Do not conform to the pattern of this world, but be transformed by the renewing of your mind. Then you will be able to test and approve what God's will is – his good, pleasing and perfect will" (Romans 12:2).

CHAPTER TWENTY-FOUR

Synodality and the Holy Spirit

In any performance, stage actors and actresses are the story*tellers*, while the audience plays the *listening* role. The storytellers and audience are like two sides of a coin. This inseparability is facilitated and managed by a stage director whose role is to create a wholesome, synergistic experience, allowing everyone to leave saying, "Did not our hearts burn within us when…?"

The Holy Spirit is the director and guide of the mission of the Church and the synodal journey. Luke clearly articulates this belief in his two-volume account, the Gospel of Luke and the Acts of the Apostles. For Luke, the Holy Spirit, the Lord and Giver of Life, initiates the earthly life and mission of Jesus and the mission of the Church. Consequently, in his gospel, he writes that:

- Jesus is conceived by the power of the Holy Spirit (1:35).

- At Mary's visit, Elizabeth is filled with the Holy Spirit (1:41).
- The Spirit descends upon Jesus like a dove at His baptism (3:22).
- The Spirit inaugurates Jesus' mission (4:16).
- Jesus hands the Spirit over to the Father upon His death (23:46).

In the Acts of the Apostles, the Spirit descends upon Mary and the disciples in the Upper Room and directs the missionary work of the early Church (2:1ff). The account of the Council of Jerusalem (Acts 15) testifies to the powerful guidance of the Holy Spirit in the Church's synodal journey. The council assembles to discuss whether Gentile converts to Christianity should undergo the Jewish ritual of circumcision as part of their initiation (15:2). At this assembly, each person is allowed to articulate their perspective.

Acts 15:5 notes one group's contribution: "Some of the believers who belonged to the party of the Pharisees stood up and said, 'The Gentiles must be circumcised and told to obey the Law of Moses'." Then, in Acts 15:6-11, the assembly listens to Peter's faith story of witnessing God's universal salvation. Finally, in Acts 15:12, Paul and Barnabas tell their own story about the miracles and wonders God had performed through them among the Gentiles.

Discerning the movement of the Spirit in the discussion, James, the council president, declares in the end: "It is my opinion that we should not trouble the Gentiles who are turning to God" (Acts 15:19). This is a scriptural example of what Cardinal Mario Grech, president of the Synod of Bishops, says in a July 2021 interview:

> To the prophetic function of the whole people of God ... corresponds the pastors' task of discernment: from what the people of God say, the pastors must grasp what the Spirit wants to say to the Church. But it is from listening to the people of God that discernment must begin. *(Tornielli)*

If the synod journey is to bear succulent spiritual fruits, the process must be characterised by the Council of Jerusalem where everyone – laity, religious, priests, and bishops – has a voice. Space ought to be created for persons or groups whose voices are usually not powerful, influential, or dominant.

Why is it essential to listen to everyone's story? By virtue of our baptism and initiation as members of the Church, we are Spirit-filled and gifted members of the Church. As members, we are on pilgrimage, on a journey, together. Therefore, everyone's story about their experience of the Holy Spirit must be told, for the people of God have "a sort of spiritual instinct that enables the believer to judge spontaneously whether a particular teaching or practice is or is not in conformity with the Gospel and with the apostolic faith" (*Sensus* #49).

The Church refers to this "spiritual instinct" as *sensus fidei*, literally translated: "sense of the faithful". Through the *sensus fidei*, the Holy Spirit enables the People of God to discern the movement of the Spirit in particular circumstances of the Church's life. To discern the movement of the Spirit, the people's stories must become like individual pieces of a puzzle which, when combined, form a universal *sense or instinct* of faith.

So, decisions are not based on a democratic or an autocratic process, nor do we move forward imprisoned by resolutions. We rely on a spirit of discernment. We ponder the question: Given all these stories, where is the Spirit leading the Church at this moment in time? Having listened to their own story and the Risen Christ's interpretation of it, the two disciples on the road to Emmaus (Luke 24:13-35) discerned that the Spirit was leading them to offer hospitality, and eventually, return to Jerusalem. May we allow the Holy Spirit to be stage director of this synodal journey.

Individual or Group Reflection

MISSIONARY CHALLENGE

So, decisions are not based on a democratic or an autocratic process, nor do we move forward imprisoned by resolutions. We rely on a spirit of discernment. We ponder the question: Given all these stories, where is the Spirit leading the Church at this moment in time?

SYNODAL EXERCISE

1. What challenges are you likely to encounter as you seek to:
    a. Share your story?
    b. Listen to others tell their story?
    c. Discern the movement of the Spirit?
2. What practices might you engage to overcome these challenges?

CHAPTER TWENTY-FIVE

Conversion and Evangelisation

The Coronavirus pandemic adversely and severely affected participation in Church life and attendance. Like the education system that lost students with the advent of online classes, the Church also suffered the loss of both active and passive members. A youth leader lamented bitterly that when parishes reopened for worship, many youths did not resume attending Mass.

With the introduction of online ministry at the start of the pandemic, pastoral leaders could not anticipate the many variables that would cause minimal or no participation. Poor quality online programming and malfunctioning equipment were common issues, as were increased competition for virtual space from secular and religious users, difficulty navigating the virtual space, poor internet connectivity in some communities, and lack of efficient devices to access online services.

Prior to the pandemic, some parishes were already losing members owing to inhospitality and irrelevant or redundant ministries. The pandemic simply fast-tracked the attrition rate. Australian theologian and missiologist, Michael Frost, wrote: "I've lost count of the number of Christians who've told me they either stopped attending church or left their church to join another one because they couldn't make any friends there" (*Lonely*).

Mindful of this augmented attrition rate, I believe the synod journey is an opportunity for *airos* – literally translated: "lift up". It is a ripe moment in the life of the Church for conversion in preparation for evangelisation. According to the synod handbook: "This Synod Process ... is intended to enable the Church to better witness to the Gospel, especially with those who live on the spiritual, social, economic, political and geographic, and existential peripheries of the world" (*Vademecum* 1.4).

Empowered and inspired by the Spirit, we are invited to relinquish our social, spiritual, economic, political, geographic, and existential comfort zones and engage those whom we have, intentionally or unintentionally, excluded or ignored. The synodal pathway prepares the Church for evangelisation. In words and actions that reflect the attitude and spirit of Jesus Christ, the Church carries out this mission.

The synodal handbook refers to some of these attitudes as "humility in listening", "courage in speaking", and "openness to ... change", "[leaving] behind prejudices and stereotypes" (2.3). This mission must be exercised intentionally, especially to those on the periphery of our own closed circles and those who have been marginalised or have marginalised themselves.

Naturally, we cannot be witnesses of someone's words and actions if we have not encountered that person and experienced conversion because of the encounter. It was the disciples' encounter with the Person and mission of Jesus Christ that triggered their personal conversion in preparation for mission.

In John's narrative of the Washing of Feet, for example, Peter's refusal to have his feet washed is greeted with an unapologetic response from Jesus: "Unless I wash you, you will have no inheritance with Me" (John 13:8). Even paraphrased, the verbal message is unblemished: "Unless you are humble enough to allow your feet to be washed by Me, you won't understand the meaning of My ministry and you can't preach in My name."

In this vein, Pope Francis and the synod secretariat have been emphasising the need for personal and communal conversion:

> "This change calls for a personal and communal conversion that makes us see things as the Lord does." [It] is an opportunity to foster the synodal and pastoral conversion of each local Church so as to be more fruitful in mission. (*Vademecum* 1.4, 1.1)

What are the necessary areas of "personal and communal conversion"? The handbook refers to them as pitfalls (2.4) or temptations to avoid. I've listed them below with associated scripture passages for your reflection:

- Wanting to lead ourselves instead of being led by God (Mark 1:36)
- Focussing on ourselves and our immediate concerns (Matthew 14:15)
- Seeing only "problems" (John 12:5)
- Focussing on structures (Acts 15:5)
- Not looking beyond the visible confines of the Church (Mark 9:38)
- Losing focus of the objectives of the synodal process (Luke 24:18)
- Conflict and division (Luke 9:46-47)
- Treating it as a kind of parliament (Acts 15:1-2)
- Listening only to those already involved in Church activities (John 6:1-15)

The synod initiative is prophetic. It arrives at a moment when the People of God – laity, religious, clergy, and bishops – need to be renewed and empowered by the Holy Spirit. We are called to mission in a constantly changing and volatile time, characterised by emotional pain, social disruption, and attrition in our worship spaces. Our response has been to lock ourselves away from each other for fear of the virus. The Holy Spirit, however, desires to unlock the gates of fear, and calls us to take the Good News to the periphery.

Individual or Group Reflection

MISSIONARY CHALLENGE

The Holy Spirit, however, desires to unlock the gates of fear, and calls us to take the Good News to the periphery.

SYNODAL EXERCISE

1. Where is this outward journey, beyond your comfort zone, likely to take you?
2. Where do you believe the Holy Spirit is calling you to spread the Good News?

CHAPTER TWENTY-SIX

Listen, Build Bridges

From the rumbling belly bottom
Of the Grenadian Kick 'Em Jenny volcano,
Caribbean voices resound in melodious song:

Listen! Let us listen.
Listen to Our Lord's call.
Listen! Let us listen.
The synodal journey has begun.

Listening to the voice of the Spirit,
Bishops from north, south,
East and west Caribbean
Traversed invisible bridges,
Crossing the Caribbean Basin,

WALKING TOGETHER

Arriving on the Antiguan land of 365 beaches.
To do what?

Listen... Listen to Our Lord's call
Crying out from the pages of synod syntheses.
To what can I liken the voice of the Holy Spirit
Reverberating from the synthesis pages?
Listen to this story:

I watched in dismay, shock, and fear
A television news report:
...school children with heavy knapsacks,
... farmers with donkey-loaded produce,
...teachers, dressed in professional attire,
Exchanging high-heeled shoes for sneakers.
. . . The elderly crawling on all fours,
. . . carefully descending a muddy, stony,
Precarious ravine.
Dancing like ballerinas on slippery rocks,
Caressed by the roaring river.
Chiselled, sculpted young men
Providing helping hands,
Saving many from drowning,
Broken bones, bruised skin.
Helping each to ascend
The other side of the valley.
Why?

LISTEN, BUILD BRIDGES

A collapsed bridge,
Crossing a major river,
Connecting villages to schools,
Police stations, farms, and shops.

Anaemic leadership is like a collapsed bridge.
There's disconnection, disorder,
Destroyed relationships.
If bridges collapse,
A Bailey bridge is a temporary replacement.
The people testified sadly,
"We are tired of Bailey bridge leadership."

From Jamaica's Blue Mountain Peak
To the Guianas' vast Amazon forests.
From the bottomless Belizean Blue Hole
To the heart of the Bermuda Triangle.
Caribbean people, holding their belly bottom,
Bawl out in labour pain,
"Build strong bridges! Resilient relationships!"

Resilient leadership connects,
Not to create uniformity,
But to accommodate healthy tensions.
Connects people,
Connects differences,

Connects diversities,
Connects ideas,
Connects perspectives,
Connects communities,
Connects spiritualities,
Connects the marginalised
To the centre.
Connects people to God's mystery.
Connects, connects, connects.

After deep intimacy with the Holy Spirit,
Bishops returned home,
Pregnant with hope,
To give birth to new relationships,
New bridges.
To repair old bridges.
To replace useless bridges.
To connect.
To build relationships.

Listen! Let us listen.
Listen to Our Lord's call.
Listen! Let us listen.
The synodal journey has begun.

Individual or Group Reflection

MISSIONARY CHALLENGE

Resilient leadership connects,
Not to create uniformity,
But to accommodate healthy tensions.

SYNODAL EXERCISE

1. In which of your relationships may you need to demonstrate more resilient leadership, the ability to recover quickly from difficult situations? What might that resilient leadership look like?
2. In your parish community relationships, where may more resilient leadership be required? Is there a story that needs to be told about this relationship?
3. What might Jesus do?

CHAPTER TWENTY-SEVEN

Synod as Listening

> For this synodal process to be enriching for both the regional and universal Church, a welcoming space must be established to listen to the people's story.
> (*Synod as Storytelling*, Fr. D. Chambers)

Luke's account of Christ's encounter and journey with two disciples (Luke 24:13-35) is a scriptural model for the synodal journey. A synod is a journey of baptised Christians sharing their stories of salvation and listening with a view to discerning the movement of the Holy Spirit in the life of the Church.

In Luke's story, we identify four movements:

1. The Risen Christ invites the disciples to tell their story of concern with the question: "What were you talking about as you walked along?"
2. The disciples emotionally tell their story.

3. Christ listens to their story.
4. Christ offers them hospitality with a meal.

The fruit of this narrative of storytelling and story-listening is a personal and pastoral decision: return to the Jerusalem community and share the story of their encounter with the Risen Christ.

Listening begins with an awareness of what's happening within me: How am I feeling and thinking? How do I rise to become – to use a term coined by Catholic author, Matthew Kelly – the "best version of myself"? In her book, *Radical Spirit*, Joan Chittister describes this awareness as realising "who we ourselves really are. We learn there what we fear and what we are resisting" (p. 159).

In *Let Us Dream*, Pope Francis refers to it using the words "decenter" and "transcend": "See where you are centered and decenter yourself. The task is to open doors and windows and move out beyond." He utilises the metaphor of a tourist versus a pilgrim. A tourist goes to the sea or mountains for relaxation but returns to a suffocating routine, while a pilgrim decenters and comes home a changed person (p. 135).

If we do not listen to our inner fears, anxieties, and/or biases, and recognise the call to transcend them, we will be unable to listen intently to someone else's story. We will find ourselves immediately analysing, based on our programmed and biased mentality, and making false judgments. Listening, therefore, begins from within ourselves and our possibilities for growth.

Armed with this interior awareness, we are prepared to listen to what is happening around us. In his book, *Rediscover the Saints*, Matthew Kelly calls it "an awareness of what is happening within the people around us. It is also an awareness of how what we do and say affect other people" (pp. 36-37).

The greatest enemy of the synodal journey is a mind that works like an automatic car that shifts quickly into the fifth gear of analysis and judgment. The synodal journey requires disengaging the "automatic" mind and re-engaging the "manual gear shift" mind, slowly embracing personal awareness. This prepares us to move into the gear of appreciating that others' stories are the gateway to knowing what's within them.

In the synodal journey of Christ and the Emmaus disciples, Christ became aware of the spiritual and emotional impact of the past on the disciples by listening to their story. He then patiently moved from attentive listening to teaching and challenging with compassion.

A potential roadblock in the path of the synodal journey is the disease of personal and cultural self-centredness. In the first chapter of *Let Us Dream*, Pope Francis writes about narcissism, discouragement, and pessimism – the three ways in which this disease manifests itself:

> Narcissism takes you to the mirror to look at yourself. ... You end up so in love with the image you created that you end up drowning in it. ... Discouragement leads you to lament and complain about everything so that you no longer see what is around you nor what others offer you, only what you think you've lost. Discouragement leads to sadness in the spiritual

life. ... Eventually, it closes you in on yourself and you can't see anything beyond yourself. [And finally,] pessimism, which is like a door you shut on the future and the new things it can hold; a door you refuse to open in case one day there'll be something new on your doorstep. (p. 15)

This self-centredness can prevent individuals, parishes, and communities from creating a hospitable space that invites others to tell their stories or even to listen to what's happening within and around them. It is only by removing ourselves from the centre that we can create a hospitable space for storytelling and story-listening.

The synodal journey is a hospitable space for stories. Every person, community, diocese, and region are invited to tell and listen to the stories of the "joys and the hopes, the griefs and the anxieties of the men of this age, especially those who are poor or in any way afflicted" (*Gaudium et Spes* #1). Storytelling and story-listening become the pathway to discerning the story of God's universal salvation.

Individual or Group Reflection

MISSIONARY CHALLENGE

The synodal journey is a hospitable space for stories. Every person, community, diocese, and region are invited to tell and listen to the stories of the "joys and the hopes, the griefs and the anxieties of the men of this age, especially those who are poor or in any way afflicted".

SYNODAL EXERCISE

1. What are the characteristics of a welcoming space?
2. What are the ways in which you currently contribute to the creation of a welcoming space?
3. What are some of the ways in which you impede/prevent the formation of a welcoming space?
4. What would help you to consistently offer a welcoming space to others?
5. What might Jesus do?

CHAPTER TWENTY-EIGHT

Historical Listening and Kairos

In a group conversation during the synod retreat for the clergy of the Archdiocese of Port of Spain, two insights related to the synodal journey emerged.

The first insight was historical listening. This type of listening is an awareness of the historical wisdom of the Church that it passes on through its living Tradition. This living Tradition is captured in the Church's official teachings, devotions, and rituals. It is also contained in the writings and witness of the People of God, especially those emerging from oppressive circumstances, such as the enslaved Africans in the Americas. In discerning the mission of the Church in the 21st century, we integrate the wisdom lessons of the past, starting with the birth of the Church on the day of Pentecost and including the Church's Jewish roots. The second insight was that the historical assemblies of the Church of the Archdiocese of Port of Spain have been *Kairos* moments. The ancient Greek word, *Kairos*, means "opportunity", "season", or "fitting time." In scripture, therefore, the word is used to mean the capacity to read the signs of the times and respond in faith. For example, Galatians 4:4-5 says, "But when the fullness of time had come, God sent forth his Son, born of a woman, born under the law, to redeem those who were under the law, so that we might receive adoption as sons."

The participants saw that these assemblies, previously believed to have been like separate waterways, now converged with the Synod 2021-2024 river to form one huge synodal river. The present, therefore, is a *Kairos* moment in the life of the local Church, to which we are all called to respond in faith.

As Joan Chittister says in *The Monastic Heart*, her book about living monastic spirituality in everyday life:

> It's not the past you seek. It is the model, the energy of the past that's important. As the poet-monk, Basho, puts it, "I do not seek to follow in the footsteps of the old. I seek the things they sought." (p. 180)

I pray that our historical listening may enable us to discern the *Kairos* moment in our midst.

Individual or Group Reflection

MISSIONARY CHALLENGE

I pray that our historical listening may enable us to discern the *Kairos* moment in our midst.

SYNODAL EXERCISE

1. As you consider previous turning points in our local Church, what opportunities might be emerging during this synodal process?
2. What might be the opportunity for personal conversion?
3. Where do you experience God's presence?

CHAPTER TWENTY-NINE

Listening to the Other

In my blog, *belovedreflections.org*, I posted an entry entitled: "Conversation, Conversation, Conversation!" Based on a weekend with two friends, I shared three wisdom lessons that emerged about healthy conversation:

- It allows you to share and receive different perspectives.
- You develop awareness of what you don't know.
- It motivates you to become more open, expansive, curious, and flexible.

Regarding the Church's synodal journey, Pope Francis invites and challenges us to engage in intentional listening, especially with two groups of persons. The handbook on the synodal process notes, "Special care should be taken to involve those persons who may risk being excluded: women, the handicapped, refugees, migrants, the elderly, people who live in poverty, Catholics who rarely or never practice their faith" (*Vademecum* 2.1).

Furthermore, as we were reminded in earlier chapters: "Fostering participation leads us out of ourselves to involve others who hold different views than we do" (*Vademecum* 2.2). For most of us, it is exceedingly difficult to adopt this open disposition to practising intentional listening by welcoming the perspectives of persons with opposing views.

We are socially and religiously hardwired to include only persons of like mind in our religious, social, ethnic, and intellectual circles. Societies are, therefore, organised with strict social stratification. Religion becomes the bedfellow of hierarchical systems offering preferential options to persons at the top of the totem pole. The logic of politics divides persons, with those who possess power having first access to the material resources of a country while the masses are utilised as stepping stones to power.

If we delve beyond a superficial interpretation of the Hebrew and Christian scriptures, we discover greater insights into Pope Francis' synodal mandate. In the Book of Job, Chapter 1, it is interesting that the writer narrates a conversation between God and Satan.

God says to Satan, "Where have you been?"

Satan responds, "Round the earth, roaming about."

God goes on. "Did you notice my servant, Job? There is no one like him on the earth: a sound and honest man who fears God and shuns evil."

Satan replies, "Yes, but Job is not God-fearing for nothing, is he?"

Why would God entertain Satan in conversation?

According to Job 1:6, Satan belongs to God's council: "One day, when the sons of God came to present themselves before the Lord, Satan also came among them."

In the Book of Job, the writer also depicts Job as welcoming, conversing with his friends who offer opposing religious beliefs as explanations for his suffering. Neither Satan's adversarial role nor the opposing opinions of Job's friends is dismissed; all are welcome and included in conversations.

What theological message can we discern from God's and Job's dispositions? American Franciscan priest and writer, Richard Rohr, reminds us of the meaning of the origin of two Greek words: "symbolic" and "diabolic". "Symbolic" means to throw together; "diabolic", to throw apart. In his book, *Job and the Mystery of Suffering*, he writes: "Evil is always dualistic, always separates: body and soul, heart from head, human from divine, masculine from feminine. Whenever we separate, evil comes into the world" (p. 42).

I believe it is never God's intention to be separated from that which God creates, despite the adversarial position of Satan, whose name translates as "adversary", or Job's friends. God's nature is to reconcile opposites. Consequently, in His ministry, Jesus Christ, who is God, chooses not only a diverse group of men as apostles, but also an adversary, Judas Iscariot, within His close circle.

Pope Francis states that the ultimate goal of the synodal journey is to forge communion among the People of God through a spirit and process of listening and discernment of the movement of the Holy Spirit. He is convinced that a powerful sign of the work of the Holy Spirit is the reconciliation of opposites: liberal and conservative, active and contemplative, young and old, rich and poor, rural and urban. In this regard, the synodal journey is a powerful manifestation of one of the pope's titles, *Pontifex Maximus*, meaning "greatest bridge-builder".

As a bridge-builder, Pope Francis' dream is that we all become bridge-builders, or reconcilers, as a result of this synodal journey. But the greatest obstacle to the bridge-building mission is the self-assured and self-righteous spirituality by which we argue: "I am right; you are wrong." This religious disposition securely places padlocks on our hearts and thinking, preventing us from exercising hospitality to persons holding opposing opinions to ours or who are outside our circle.

This synodal journey, therefore, calls for conversion, breaking us down so we discover and learn a fresh and deeper definition of God who communes with all, even an adversary, in conversation. To what end?

Rohr writes: "I think this will be the final revelation of God's greatness, that God somehow uses evil and suffering in our favor" (p. 44). Let us not fear differences, then, but be courageous enough to engage in intentional listening.

Individual or Group Reflection

MISSIONARY CHALLENGE

This synodal journey, therefore, calls for conversion, breaking us down so we discover and learn a fresh and deeper definition of God who communes with all, even an adversary, in conversation.

SYNODAL EXERCISE

1. Reach out to someone who consistently has opposing opinions to yours or who is outside your own circle.
2. Practice listening to them in a manner that demonstrates interest and allows them to feel valued.
3. Ask the Holy Spirit for guidance. Ponder Ephesians 4:29:

    "Don't use foul or abusive language. Let everything you say be good and helpful, so that your words will be an encouragement to those who hear them."

CHAPTER THIRTY

Reception of Ideas

The synodal journey is one of dialogue, discernment, and decision-making by the People of God. One of the most frustrating experiences is having a proposed idea, concept, or recommendation shot immediately down, thrown instantaneously in the garbage. There may be good reasons for rejection, but the manner in which it is done without considering the possibility of there being an iota of truth to it is unpleasant and potentially offensive.

In the consultative phase of the synod, a participant spoke of "decision-making being made at the top" and "no systems in place to allow persons to share ideas except directly to the priest". No one person or group has the solutions to life's challenges. It is the contribution of the individual to the whole that produces suitable responses.

Letters form words, words form sentences. Sentences form paragraphs, paragraphs form chapters. Chapters form a book, books form a collection of stories, a collection of stories forms a library. And libraries form a diversity of stories, ideas, concepts, beliefs, and philosophies.

The tendency to dominate is a human challenge. The dominant utilises intellectual, religious, emotional, physical, and social resources to intimidate, oppress, and repress – in a word, to exercise ultimate control. The dominated are then deprived of their worth and value. They're also deprived of their freedom because, when the weight of dominance lies heavy on them, they must channel precious resources towards one purpose only – to watch their backs.

The synodal journey invites everyone to value the diversity of letters, words, sentences, paragraphs, chapters, books, and libraries available to us. As one participant of the synodal journey remarked, "The Synod provides the opportunity for Catholics to verbalise their thoughts and ideas. The Church now has the opportunity to listen to the voices of its people."

When an idea, concept, or plan is proposed, first acknowledge and express gratitude for the contribution and value the effort. Articulate your feelings and thoughts when you read it, and then, make your own proposal. The synodal journey invites us to resist the shoot-down approach and develop the ability to listen, evaluate, and respond together in the process of discernment and decision making. Remember, the goal is discerning God's will for the present.

Individual or Group Reflection

MISSIONARY CHALLENGE

The synodal journey invites us to resist the shoot-down approach and develop the ability to listen, evaluate, and respond together in the process of discernment and decision making.

SYNODAL EXERCISE

1. As you engage in discussions on what is emerging in the synodal conversations, be conscious of tendencies to categorise contributions as "right or wrong", or "I agree or disagree", and tendencies to begin your responses with the word "but".
2. What happens when you choose to adopt a posture of curiosity?
3. What do you think the Holy Spirit is saying to you?

CHAPTER THIRTY-ONE

Bridle & Bit Discipline

My Dad tells the story of his childhood donkey named Aaron. True to the conduct expected of a donkey, Aaron was stubborn and incredibly wild. He was, therefore, primarily controlled by placing a bridle and bit on his mouth.

The bit is a metal bar placed behind the teeth, resting against the soft tissues in the back of the mouth. It is controlled by the bridle, which is operated by the reins. Each time Aaron's wildness erupted, the bridle activated the bit which squeezed his tongue. So painful!

Discipline of the tongue is needed by the People of God on the synodal journey. The tongue is an extraordinary gift of God to be used for communication and for initiating and nurturing relationships. On the synodal journey, communication with the tongue is vitally important. Depending on the quality of communication, the tongue can enhance or break down relationships, and thus, community life.

In the Letter of James 3:1-12, the writer says the tongue is the most difficult part of the body to control. The one who controls his or her words, therefore, controls the entire body. James utilises the metaphor of the bridle as a means of controlling the body. He says the horse is a powerful animal, and yet, can be controlled with a small piece of metal – the bit – and leather straps. The power of the bit is not its size, but the effectiveness of its control.

On the synodal journey, there is a need to develop discipline of the tongue, learning the wisdom of what to communicate, how to communicate it, and the appropriate time to communicate. This is what I refer to as bridle and bit discipline. It is the ongoing formation of learning to use the gift of speech to communicate with God and to affirm, uplift, challenge, teach, and care for each other on the synodal journey.

Individual or Group Reflection

MISSIONARY CHALLENGE

On the synodal journey, there is a need to develop discipline of the tongue, learning the wisdom of what to communicate, how to communicate it, and the appropriate time to communicate. This is what I refer to as bridle and bit discipline.

SYNODAL EXERCISE

1. How do your friends describe your way of communicating?
2. Are you able to balance speaking your truth with care and support for the other?
3. "There is one whose rash words are like sword thrusts, but the tongue of the wise brings healing" (Proverbs 12:18). Call on the Holy Spirit for guidance that your words will, indeed, bring healing.

CHAPTER THIRTY-TWO

Synodal Eyes

Along with scores of Thanksgiving Day passengers, I stood anxiously awaiting the arrival of my luggage on the conveyor belt. A Miami airport worker arrived with a young man in a wheelchair and stopped about six feet to my right. Clearly a patient, and victim, of an orthopaedic surgeon, the dreadlocked Afro-looking young man had a pair of crutches at his left like swords. His right leg, the obviously wounded one, was straight as an arrow.

An older man darted from my left, passing between myself and the conveyor belt. He approached the young man and initiated a conversation. While not privy to the words of the conversation, their body language communicated that they were speaking about the wounded leg.

Sitting in the wheelchair, the young man's torso was perpendicular to the conveyor belt, his head slightly upturned. When he nodded, the movements were deliberate, slow. He spoke only occasionally; his was a disposition of listening.

As he listened to the stranger, his eyes caught my attention. At first, I could see only one of them. It was focussed, attentive, piercing as he gently absorbed the words of the stranger. I could then see both eyes. They were relaxed ovals, not wide open in surprise, fright, or shock. Standing in awe, my mind whispered, "Look at those synodal eyes."

I prayed for the grace to participate in the Church's synodal journey with the eyes of this young man.

Individual or Group Reflection

MISSIONARY CHALLENGE

His was a disposition of listening. Standing in awe, my mind whispered, "Look at those synodal eyes."

SYNODAL EXERCISE

1. As you engage in this synodal journey, what would you have to be or do to help you listen more attentively to others? What might make the other person know that you are listening to them attentively?
2. What would you have to be or do to help you listen to and discern more clearly the voice of God?.

CHAPTER THIRTY-THREE

Synod as Storytelling

The word "synod" originates from the Greek word *sunodos*; *sun* means "together" and *hodos* means "way" or "road". In essence, it means "common road". Hence, you will often hear the expressions "synodal process" or "ecclesial journey"; "ecclesial" means "relating to the Church". So, a synod is not a one-time event. It is an ongoing ecclesial journey.

What does the Church do on a journey? Addressing members of the International Theological Commission in 2019 (Wooden, *Not a Walk*), Pope Francis said:

> Today some think synodality is holding hands and going for a walk, having a party with young people or surveying opinions (like), "What do you think about women priests?" Rather, it's a process that involves the whole church and focuses on listening to one another and to the inspiration of the Holy Spirit. (Francis, *Audience*)

If, as the Holy Father says, listening is essential to this synodal journey "so that the wisdom of the people of God will come forth" (Wooden), then the process must value and accommodate the people's art of storytelling. As George Wilson writes in the June 2021 issue of *La Croix International*:

> The first thing a synod needs to ask of its participants ... is not to ask, "what do you *think* about *abc*?" But ... "Tell me your story." To ask about "*abc*" is to assume at the outset that *abc* is the issue people need or want to discuss when, in fact, deeper realities may be at stake.

Each person is a social being with the capacity for self-awareness. A story is defined as an account of past events in someone's or a community's life or in the development of something. Using this definition, then, we can say that every person, community, family, nation, or region has stories to tell.

In his book, *Existentialism*, Scottish theologian, John Macquarrie, says that, as social beings, we are rooted in a particular culture and historical milieu, and we shape and influence our basic activities and orientation to this world (pp. 48-86). It is in the shaping and influencing of our world that stories are created.

The peoples of the Caribbean, for example, have stories arising from the shaping of their historical experience during slavery, indentureship, Emancipation, colonialism, and Independence. Regrettably, the history of the Caribbean demonstrates that dominant cultures have the tendency, or the mission, to suppress, misrepresent, or misinterpret the stories of weaker civilisations.

What is the purpose of storytelling? Storytelling reflects on the past, provides wisdom lessons for the present, and carves out a community's road to the future. Storytelling reinforces and celebrates a person's or community's identity, building unity around a set of common values. It is a vehicle for transmitting values.

Storytelling breathes confidence and courage into communities, stirring them to action. Aware of its power, slave masters in the Caribbean enacted legislation to prohibit the African slaves from gathering, speaking their languages, practising their religions, and playing their drums. They feared these storytelling forms could incite the enslaved to revolt and liberation.

If the synodal journey involves attentive listening to each other and to the Holy Spirit, then the Church has a responsibility to create a safe, welcoming, and inclusive space. Creating this safe space consists of asking open-ended questions, rather than questions garbed in ulterior motives.

The Risen Christ, in His approach to the two disciples on the Emmaus road (Luke 24:13-35), gives an example of initiating a safe space. He asked them a non-threatening, open-ended, and non-conceptual question: "What are you talking about as you walk along?" His question inspired freedom in the disciples. They could tell their story of the Jesus of Nazareth who was considered a prophet, His death by crucifixion, their hopes for the liberation of Israel, His missing body, and the empty tomb.

What is the story of the Caribbean people? We have emerged from hybrid societies with global cultural and religious roots. There is a full reservoir of stories that speaks implicitly and explicitly of God's journey with us, captured in many genres by poets, artists, musicians, storytellers, and literary writers.

I believe the synod is an opportune moment for the Caribbean Church to encourage people to tell their stories using the native language and literary forms of the people to discern God's "right hand writing in our land". For this synodal process to be enriching for both the regional and universal Church, a welcoming space must be established to welcome and listen to the people's story.

Individual or Group Reflection

MISSIONARY CHALLENGE

I believe the synod is an opportune moment for the Caribbean Church to encourage people to tell their stories using the native language and literary forms of the people to discern God's "right hand writing in our land".

SYNODAL EXERCISE

1. What would encourage you to tell your story in your community?
2. How might you include the local culture – music, art, dance, et cetera – as you share your story?
3. What is the Holy Spirit prompting you to share?

CHAPTER THIRTY-FOUR

Synod Response

In the third week of Lent 2022, I preached a retreat in the Catholic Church's Toco missions of Rampanalgas, Cumana, Mission, Grand Riviere, and Matelot. I reflected on the theme, "Synod: Communion, Participation, and Mission."

In response to this time of reflection, two attendees from the Cumana Parish, Rebecca Francis and Nicole Richards-Bishop, crafted a prayer and two poems, respectively, on the synod. We share them below.

PRAYER
by Rebecca Francis

Lord Jesus, we pray ... for a pure heart, one to respond to each other with compassion and mercy, to participate in sharing our own story. Help us to build confidence and faith [in] sharing our very own story.

We pray too, O God, that each chapter in our story of broken and wounded hearts would be healed. [We] pray ... for forgiveness so that we may open our hearts to accepting your blessings and grace. Bend our hearts to your will in communion, participation, and mission.

And we pray for that space, O God, to share our messiness without others being judgmental. We ask all this through Christ our Lord. Amen.

MY SYNOD STORY
by Nicole Richards-Bishop

You want me to tell you my story!
For people to gossip about me!
You want me to tell you my story,
And tell it willingly and freely!
I don't know what herb you're smoking!
You say it is a synodal thinking.
To have a space to share our experiences,
A whole new change must invade our senses.
We must listen,
And not be judgmental.
Reach out to someone,
It is essential.

SYNOD RESPONSE

TOCO TALK
by Nicole Richards-Bishop

This little bacchanalist came to town,
Telling us to give we story and is onward bound!
He boldly say to dig deeper today.
Well now ah sweating,
More than if I was digging yam whole day!
So mouth continue to open,
And Synod came out.
"Communion, Participation, and Mission," was his shout!
He came by my ear,
Well, I start to get frighten!
He say yuh using this to hear,
But yuh need to listen!

He continued to give some practical activities.
To be aware of our thoughts and all the nitty gritties.
To let our feelings go!
Well, I thought I was Elsa!
You know the Frozen princess?
Yes! That Disney character!

He said to listen to others,
Let them tell their whole story.
Pocket your opinions,

WALKING TOGETHER

Don't "mash up" the party!
Look out for discernment,
There must be a common thread,
I only realised it wasn't the sewing kind,
Just before I reached in my bed.

Well, oh gosh, he bring down the house!
When he talk about gossiping!
He say stop the eavesdropping and the macoing!
Well, this Jamaican man,
Real had we up in we feelings.
Go to the source people,
Don't take no second-hand helpings.
And as we sat in his Chambers,
He continued to flow!
You know who I'm talking about!
Yuh don' know?

Individual or Group Reflection

MISSIONARY CHALLENGE

He said to listen to others,
Let them tell their whole story.
Pocket your opinions,
Don't "mash up" the party!
Look out for discernment,
There must be a common thread,
I only realised it wasn't the sewing kind,
Just before I reached in my bed.

SYNODAL EXERCISE

1. "Be anxious for nothing" (Philippians 4:6-7). How do you bring this scripture to life?
2. What are your fears and anxieties around sharing your story?
3. How might others help you to overcome these fears?
4. What might you do to make others feel safe to share their story?

CHAPTER THIRTY-FIVE

Waiting

Have you ever had the experience of waiting on a response from someone? On your boss' reaction to a project proposal, for instance, or your parents' reply to a request. Waiting on responses to a love note to a girl or boyfriend, a submitted application form, or an invitation you sent.

Waiting belongs to a liminal space, a between and betwixt space, a space of vulnerability. A space in which control and predictability are arrested. It's a space in which you anticipate a verbal or active response. This space ranges from the short time-space of greeting someone and receiving their immediate reply, to the long time-space of writing someone a critical note and looking out for an answer.

Waiting is a dark, yet transformable, space; dark because the bright lights of control and predictability are extinguished. You are alone in the space, not knowing where to turn, what to do, or how to move forward. It is like the tomb of a dead body awaiting the resurrection of someone's response – a response that may or may not arise. Whatever happens, we use this liminal moment as one of transformation, allowing it to emotionally empower us, rather than emasculate.

Just as dialogue and discernment are crucial to the synodal journey, so understanding the nature and spirituality of waiting is similarly central. Waiting is that space between the ebb of an initiative, such as sharing, and the flow of someone's response.

Occasionally, the timing of responses is unpredictable; they may be immediate or delayed, and many factors determine the rate of response. Personality types, for example, could influence the way in which a person receives or understands the initiative. Other practical circumstances, such as unavailability or malfunction of the means of communication, could also delay responses. In that timespace, we may sometimes ask: "Where is my God?"

Whatever the circumstances, if there's an ebb, synodal participation requires a flow. A poor or perennial lack of response can be likened to destroying a bridge, or building an inadequate one, for connecting the two sides of a valley. Waiting may offer opportunities for growth for the People of God, but permanent waiting stalls the movement of the synodal journey.

Individual or Group Reflection

MISSIONARY CHALLENGE

Just as dialogue and discernment are crucial to the synodal journey, so understanding the nature and spirituality of waiting is similarly central. Waiting is that space between the ebb of an initiative, such as sharing, and the flow of someone's response.

SYNODAL EXERCISE

Invite your partner to respond to the question: "What are your expectations of this synodal journey?" Allow five minutes for the response.

1. During the five-minute response period, be content to not ask any further questions and to accept whatever periods of silence may occur.
2. Be aware of the emotions you are experiencing and how the Holy Spirit may be speaking to you.
3. At the end of the five-minute period, share the experience with your partner, then swap roles.

CHAPTER THIRTY-SIX

Conflict Transformation

The synodal journey fundamentally involves the initiation and development of quality relationships. Relationship building entails occasionally getting under another's skin which, naturally, results in conflict.

There's no synodal journey without conflict. It emerges naturally, often owing to differences in personality, experience, perspectives, opinions, ways of communicating, and intentions. Yet, some participants at the diocesan phase of the synodal journey describe conflict as "uncomfortable and messy", but fruitful.

It is the courage to be vulnerable and the utilisation of the necessary spiritual and human tools for navigating conflicts that make the synodal journey fruitful. In *Braving the Wilderness*, this is referred to as "conflict transformation". Brené Brown offers some tips on this skill from an interview with Dr. Michelle Buck (pp. 69-72).

First – it is essential to avoid the "agree to disagree", "silent treatment", or "withdrawal" approaches for the sake of peace. This only opens the door to making assumptions about others and deepens misunderstanding, leading to further resentment. To learn more about the other party, difficult conversations need to be had; this opens the door to mutual understanding and mutual respect.

Second – aim to make our underlying intentions explicit. What is the conversation about? What do we want for our parish or family? Expressed intentions build mutual connections.

Third – avoid the temptation to turn the conversation into a court case in which there is examination and cross examination. Shift the focus to the "now" and the "future." In going forward, what do we want our relationship to be? Even if we disagree, what do we need to do to create this future?

Fourth – the conversation ought to be about conflict transformation and not conflict resolution. Conflict transformation is creatively navigating the conversational space, marked by differences and disagreements, towards creating something new by learning about each other.

Finally, fifth – there is a need to slow things down in a conflict by listening with the desire to learn more about the other person's perspective. Phrases such as: "Tell me more", "I don't fully understand", and "Help me to understand why it is so important to you" can develop this clarity.

The synodal journey is about discerning, dialoguing, and decision-making together. Therefore, conflict transformation is an essential human tool for all participants.

Individual or Group Reflection

MISSIONARY CHALLENGE

The synodal journey is about discerning, dialoguing, and decision-making together. Therefore, conflict transformation is an essential human tool for all participants.

SYNODAL EXERCISE

Reflect on some of the recent conflicts you have had.

1. Was your position one of seeking to: (a) agree to disagree, (b) understand the other, (c) convince the other that you were right, (d) be silent, or (e) withdraw?
2. How might the outcome of the conflict been different had you adopted a conflict transformation approach, seeking to discover more about the other?
3. What was Jesus' posture when faced with conflict?

CHAPTER THIRTY-SEVEN

Frustration

The feeling of frustration is one of the many emotions that people either express or intuit as they share their stories during the consultation phase of the synodal journey. I'm sure you can sense the frustration in the following testimony extracted from a synod synthesis:

> Some of the priests are very thin-skinned and think that any comment about how we can do better is a direct personal attack. But our priests need feedback too. They are not perfect, and a very sensitive or arrogant priest can spoil it for everyone. You can be ostracised by the Church if you have an opinion that's opposite to Church teaching… If we can ever get to a stage where persons can share differing points of view and have healthy debate around emotional topics, then this will encourage persons to be more candid.

Frustration is like travelling in a boat on the high seas, being tossed helplessly about by turbulent waves and gusty, stinging winds. It is a feeling of being upset or annoyed as a result of being unable to change or achieve something.

The People of God experience something similar as they engage in the process of listening, discerning, and decision-making. It's an overwhelming, almost uncontrollable, situation that requires refined navigational skills until conditions change. So, how do we navigate the emotions of frustration on the synodal journey?

The synodal experience provides an opportunity for the People of God to freely share about their experience of walking together as Church in their respective parishes, communities, or dioceses. Perhaps many persons had buried those feelings for numerous years due to the lack of opportunities to share them. Others may have remained silent about past traumas in an attempt to protect them from further hurts.

The synodal experience facilitates the opening of a Pandora's box, an opportunity simply to off-load about inhospitality, voicelessness, neglect, or being ignored. Off-loading produces interior calm, as the disciples on their way to Emmaus discovered (Luke 24:13-35). When we experience this calm, the next phase of the synodal journey offers a space of ongoing discernment and decision-making.

We need to have the courage to tell our stories of frustration. The Church, therefore, has a responsibility to prepare a space of trust and listening in which the People of God can share them. Sharing and listening to difficult stories are basic tools for navigating the rough seas of frustration on the synodal journey.

Individual or Group Reflection

MISSIONARY CHALLENGE

We need to have the courage to tell our stories of frustration. The Church, therefore, has a responsibility to prepare a space of trust and listening in which the People of God can share them.

SYNODAL EXERCISE

1. Draw something that represents your story of frustration with our Church.
2. What is the key source of your frustration?
3. How do you feel having shared your frustration?
4. What would release your frustration?
5. Where is God in your frustration?

CHAPTER THIRTY-EIGHT

Solitude

I fondly remember summer hikes with my childhood church community in the hills and mountains of St. Andrew, Jamaica. With joy and excitement, I always anticipated the summer months and their rituals: the preparation of food and gear, the sleepless night before the hike, the assembly of youth and altar server groups at the meeting point, the roll call, and of course, the actual event!

The day was filled with joy, anguish, and sorrow, born of injury and sundry experiences. Competition was high. Everybody was eager to see who would be first at the finish line. The exhilaration of arrival merged with the woeful aftermath of terrible aches and pains.

Along the journey, I would, periodically and briefly, separate myself from the crowd, pausing to admire plants, flowers, steep precipices. I simply needed a break from the noise of the group, to play with my own thoughts. I learnt the value of solitude on these hikes.

Solitude gives space for inner listening to our feelings and thoughts, to our fears and dreams. In *The Monastic Heart*, Joan Chittister reminds us that solitude, or separation from others, is not an escape from life. She writes:

[A]s scripture puts it, 'Go apart for a while' that you get to know yourself. You find out, if you'll listen, exactly what it is that is driving you. You also find out what it is that is weighing you down... (pp. 98-99)

While the synodal journey is about a community walking together, it is individual spiritual development that nourishes and allows one to contribute to the communal journey. Solitude is key to this spiritual development. It can be likened to the withdrawal of individual trees in the dry season. They lose their leaves in the dry season and regain them in the wet to contribute to the growth of the forest.

Just as Jesus took time away from the communal journey, each participant is called to seek God and self in solitude in order to seek God in communion.

Individual or Group Reflection

MISSIONARY CHALLENGE

While the synodal journey is about a community walking together, it is individual spiritual development that nourishes and allows one to contribute to the communal journey. Solitude is key to this spiritual development.

SYNODAL EXERCISE

1. Do you have a spiritual practice of solitude, drawing away from the crowds?
2. What has been your experience with periods of solitude?
3. What might be the impact of including this practice in your synodal journey?

CHAPTER THIRTY-NINE

Contributing to the Whole

God acts in the simplicity of open hearts, in the patience of those who pause until they can see clearly.
(Pope Francis, *Let Us Dream*)

The rhythm of one's heart is an indicator of overall wellness. To discern a patient's state of health, a doctor will listen intently to their heart with a stethoscope. Listening is so important that the physician places the stethoscope's earpieces into his or her ears to exclude distracting environmental sounds.

Similarly, on the synodal journey, listening to the Holy Spirit is essential in discerning God's will. Indeed, the quality of communal discernment relies heavily on individual participants' ability to listen. Each participant, therefore, needs to engage in spiritual listening in order to contribute to communal listening. It is much like cooperative farming – the group's overall success depends largely on the quality of the fruit each member farmer brings to the organisation.

Participants in the synodal journey need to visit the chapel of their hearts often to listen to the Spirit who comes in a "gentle whisper" (1 Kings 19:12). In Matthew 6:6, disciples of Christ are invited to: "Go into your room, close the door and pray ... in secret." This room in which we pray in secret is the silence of the heart. It is a sacred place; this is where God is waiting in our broken lives.

Many disciples do not have ready access to a physical chapel each day, but every disciple has immediate access to his or her own heart where God awaits them. A visit to the chapel of our heart is essential. In *The Monastic Heart*, Joan Chittister reminds us that, "What we give time to creates us" (p. 149).

It costs nothing to travel to our interior chapel, only awareness and the willingness to pause for a few moments during the day and listen – to use St. Francis' imagery – with "the ear of the heart" (Francis, *Listening*).

If we give time to silent listening to the Spirit, we become discerning disciples. Listening and discerning disciples form listening and discerning communities. Listening to the heart is a vital skill in creating a healthy society.

> "In every beating heart is a silent undercurrent
> that calls each of us to the more of ourselves."
> (Joan Chittister, *The Monastic Heart*)

Individual or Group Reflection

MISSIONARY CHALLENGE

Listening to the Holy Spirit is essential in discerning God's will. Each participant, therefore, needs to engage in spiritual listening in order to contribute to communal listening.

SYNODAL EXERCISE

Meditation (15 minutes):

Sit still with your back straight. Lightly close your eyes. Interiorly recite a single prayer word or mantra. We recommend the ancient Christian prayer word: Maranatha. Say the word with equal emphasis on its four syllables: "Ma-ra-na-tha".

Breathe normally, giving your full attention to the word as you say it silently, gently, and above all, simply.

Stay with the same word during the entire meditation. Don't visualise the word; *listen* to it as you say it. Continue to use this same word in each of your daily meditation sessions: "Ma-ra-na-tha".

Let go of all images, other words, and thoughts – even good ones. Still distracted? Return to your word as soon as you realise you have stopped saying it or when your attention wanders. Don't fight distractions, release them by saying your word faithfully, gently, and attentively.

CHAPTER FORTY

Conversion

Nature teaches fundamental wisdom lessons.
Growth occurs by shedding or dismantling the old,
Allowing the new to emerge.

Snakes shed old skin,
Trees shed dried leaves.
Animals shed old fur,
Humans shed old nails, skin, hair.
Newness erupts when the old surrenders.

"To insist on the spiritual practice that served you in the past is to carry the raft on your back after you have crossed the river." – Buddha

WALKING TOGETHER

Synodality is a call to a NEW WAY of being Church:
to journey together,
to listen together,
to discern together,
to decide together,
to plan together,
to implement together,
to evaluate together.

But the old needs shedding,
the old, false masks.
What's the old?
The old is what's harming us:
The clerical model of Church
Seen as the privileged clergy's holiest power,
To lead in front, while the laity follow
Like the enslaved on a sugar plantation.
The clerical model has brought harm to everyone,
Even to those who exercise it.

"[O]nce you understand the harm you have done to others, as well as yourself, you are on the verge of becoming the person you are meant to be." – Joan Chittister, *The Monastic Heart* (p. 73).

When leaves become dry, fall, and wither away, this is a sign of the times, an indication that the dry season has come.

The clerical model of the Church can be compared to these trees, this synodal time to the dry season.

In this synodal dry season, this sign of the times, the leafless tree of the clerical model of Church waits with anticipation for new leaves, for a new model to spring forth. It's a time of conversion.

Individual or Group Reflection

MISSIONARY CHALLENGE

In this synodal dry season, this sign of the times, the leafless tree of the clerical model of Church waits in anticipation for new leaves, for a new model to spring forth.

SYNODAL EXERCISE

Prayer:
Heavenly Father, change is always difficult, even when what it promises is better than what we have in hand. As we make this synodal journey, I pray for a willingness to let go of what no longer serves, and embrace all that is required for full conversion. I ask this in Jesus' name. Amen.

After reciting the prayer, spend five minutes in silence, discerning what the Holy Spirit may be laying on your heart.

CHAPTER FORTY-ONE

Ego

Decision-making occurs in the factory of the mind
And is informed by the spirituality of the heart.
According to Sigmund Freud,
There are three interactive pieces:
   the id, the ego, and the superego.

The ego is like a bridge:
   Visible
   Architecturally creative
   Aesthetically beautiful
   Mechanically innovative.
We see evidence of the ego
   in our actions and interactions
      with the environment, people, self, and God.

WALKING TOGETHER

The bridge is anchored,
Never stands alone.
Like hands, on either side of the bridge,
Two separate landmasses hold it in place.

On one side, there's the landmass of the id.
On the other, the landmass of the superego.
Id initiates a conversation, saying,
  "I am hungry!"
  "I am sexually aroused now!"
  "I must have leadership power now!"

The superego responds:
  "I am in the middle of a meeting; it's not the right time to eat!"
  "I can't have sexual interaction; it's inappropriate!"
  "I can't instigate a *coup d'état* because…!"

Ego, the bridge, then breathes a sigh of relief, and says:
  "How do I manage my hunger?"
  "How do I manage my ravenous sex drive?"
  "How do I manage my hunger for power?"

Id is the instinctive and primitive drive.
Superego is the moral conscience.
Ego is the decision maker – the bridge.

EGO

When the superego is spiritually and intellectually malformed,
Ego, the bridge, weakens.
Then, the ego:

separates rather than unites,
stands alone rather than in communion,
dominates rather than collaborates,
journeys alone rather than together,
stands on top rather than with,
desires competition rather than participation,
becomes destiny-focussed rather than experience-focussed,
manipulates and controls rather than invites,
becomes boastful rather than humble,
leads in front and forgets those behind,
excludes the weak and vulnerable rather than include,
leads with colourful words rather than with humble action,
abandons the fallen rather than walk with them,
hardens the heart rather than opens it to listen,
makes self-decisions rather than discern with others,
and confuses colourful religious garbs and authority for authentic spirituality.

A well informed and formed superego inspires
Communion, Participation, and Mission together.

Individual or Group Reflection

MISSIONARY CHALLENGE

A well informed and formed superego inspires Communion, Participation, and Mission together.

SYNODAL EXERCISE

1. What practices may help you develop a well-formed superego?
2. What might you do to facilitate its ongoing development?
3. Where in scripture was Jesus' ego challenged? How did He respond?

CHAPTER FORTY-TWO

Dance of the Kairos and Chronos

Synodality is communication,
> listening, discerning, deciding, implementing, planning, evaluating TOGETHER.
> Think of listening, discerning, deciding, implementing, planning, evaluating as beads on a string – the string of communication.

Communication is like a dance,
> a dance between two partners,
> *Kairos* and *Chronos*.

Kairos moves to an internal rhythm,
> a rhythm deep in our souls.
> *Kairos* lives in the present moment,
> awareness of the NOW.

Kairos is sensitive
> to the feelings, thoughts, and actions of each member of the group.

Kairos befriends silence to listen,
> listen from where the Spirit is blowing.

Kairos reads the "signs of the times" and responds in faith:
> "The meeting is scheduled to begin now. However…!"

Chronos moves to an external rhythm,
> a rhythm of measurable time.

Chronos lives in the future moment,
> awareness of the destination.

Chronos is sensitive
> to goals and objectives.

Chronos befriends function,
> the activities that need to be done.

Chronos is measured, ticking, quantitative time,
> "The meeting MUST begin on time, come what may."

Without *Kairos, Chronos* becomes the slave master of quantitative time,
> driving persons with the whip of goals, objectives, deadlines,

> placing projects and programmes before the dignity of persons.

Without *Chronos, Kairos* becomes the proverbial dog chasing its own tail,
> meandering in the desert,
> exhausted by repetition.

The *Kairos* and the *Chronos* in us
> learn to dance TOGETHER,
> respect each other,
> collaborate with each other,
> value each other.

In listening, discerning, deciding, implementing, planning, evaluating,
> *Kairos* and *Chronos* learn to communicate,
> to dance the dance of the journey,
> to dance the dance of TIME.
> Holding the beads together.
> Finding the *Kairos* in the *Chronos* moment,
> Finding the *Chronos* in the *Kairos* moment.

Individual or Group Reflection

MISSIONARY CHALLENGE

The *Kairos* and the *Chronos* in us
    learn to dance TOGETHER,
    respect each other,
    collaborate with each other,
    value each other.

SYNODAL EXERCISE

1. Which partner do you tend to favour, *Kairos* or *Chronos*?
2. What might you need to do to develop a more collaborative relationship between *Kairos* and *Chronos*?
3. How might a more collaborative relationship assist you with your synodal journey?

CHAPTER FORTY-THREE

Synod Thoughts: Pope Francis & Brené Brown

The voice of the Holy Spirit speaks loudly through the words of two persons, thousands of miles apart – a religious leader and a grounded qualitative theory researcher. Ponder these words!

> The world feels high lonesome and heart-broken to me right now. ... We've turned away from one another and toward blame and rage. We're lonely and untethered. ... [R]ather than coming together and sharing our experiences through song and story, we're screaming at one another from further and further away. Rather than dancing and praying together, we're running from one another. Rather than pitching wild and innovative new ideas that could potentially change everything, we're staying quiet and small

in our bunkers and loud in our echo chambers. (Brené Brown, *Braving the Wilderness*, p. 42)

We need a movement of people who know we need each other, who have a sense of responsibility to others and to the world. We need to proclaim that being kind, having faith, and working for the common good are great life goals that need courage and vigor. Fraternity will enable freedom and equality to take its rightful place in the symphony. (Pope Francis, *Let Us Dream: The Path to a Better Future*, p. 7)

Individual or Group Reflection

MISSIONARY CHALLENGE

"We're lonely and untethered. ... [R]ather than coming together and sharing our experiences through song and story, we're screaming at one another from further and further away."

SYNODAL EXERCISE

1. In what areas of your life – family, work, neighbourhood, Church – are there people from whom you have been distancing yourself?
2. How might you seek to reengage with them during this synodal journey?
3. What support might you need to begin this process?
4. How did Jesus encourage inclusion? What is the Holy Spirit asking of you in these relationships?

CHAPTER FORTY-FOUR

Jigsaw Puzzle: Metaphor for the Synodal Journey

In a jigsaw puzzle, each piece has a different shape, a different contour, a different colour. The pieces lie jumbled together in the box, waiting to be opened and spread out on the table.

Each piece of a jigsaw puzzle represents a human story – that of a lay person, a cleric, a bishop. We are all jumbled together in the box of life, waiting to be opened and spread out on the table. In the dark and confined box of individuality, there is no meaning, no value, no purpose.

Synod is the moment God opens the box, spreads out all the pieces of the puzzle on the table of life. Alone, each piece is like a fish out of water: helpless, lifeless, of no use at all. Each piece is a story, an incomplete story, an unfinished symphony that only has significance when it's put together with the whole. Slowly, meticulously, and very patiently, God works night and day to match the pieces together.

It takes time. Like the story of the earth, of humans and societies, it takes days, weeks, months, years, decades, centuries – millions and billions of years to unfold. As the pieces are placed together, gradually, the story of the whole begins to be revealed. But the revelation is not without a painful and challenging process.

Some pieces are hidden under others. Other pieces seem to resemble each other. Still others may be missing – fallen to the ground or accidently misplaced.

Methodically, faithfully, God works, searching, finding every piece, putting them together, because each piece is important, but incomplete on its own. The story of the one becomes significant by simply being part of the whole. The journey becomes complete when every piece has found its unique place in the whole; the attractive, the ugly, the small, the large, the crooked all have a place. Only when every piece finds its place in the whole is the story of the whole revealed.

Everyone is a piece of that puzzle. Each of us has a significant place in the whole.

Make yourself available to the whole, and its beauty will be revealed.

Individual or Group Reflection

MISSIONARY CHALLENGE

Each piece is a story, an incomplete story, an unfinished symphony that only has significance when it's put together with the whole. Slowly, meticulously, and very patiently, God works night and day to match the pieces together.

SYNODAL EXERCISE

1. Reflect on your story. Draw something that symbolises it.
2. Give three (3) key words that describe what your drawing represents.
3. Where in your story do you most experience God's presence?

CHAPTER FORTY-FIVE

Synod Journey to Matelot

The synod journey is like a drive on a winding, narrow, pothole-riddled, rural road. Fr. Raymond Francis, Fr. Peter St. Hillaire, and I were once on such a journey – a relaxed drive along the coast from the village of Mission to Matelot in Trinidad.

Car windows down, we were caressed by the natural air-conditioning of coastal breeze, green scenery, and the roaring of ocean waves. Water-filled potholes disturbed us only intermittently.

The journey involved conversation about pastoral ministry and personal lives – "ole talk". Not gossiping, complaining, or grumbling. Fr. Peter drove at a snail's pace through villages such as Anse Noir, Grand Riviere, and St. Helena. As he passed, waving to persons in the squares, he shared a brief history of each area. We visited the Catholic churches and stopped to take pics.

In the village of Matelot, we disembarked at the foundation of the old church and the abandoned, dilapidated presbytery located on a short narrow street named Sr. Rosario Street. Sr. Rosario Hackshaw, CHF, pastored extensively in Matelot; the fruits of her labour were the Matelot R.C. School and the Matelot Secondary School. With this information, I asked myself, "What will be **my** legacy? What will be the fruits of my labour?"

One exhilarating stage of the journey was a swim in Shark River. Yes! Shark River! Without the sharks. Legend, or history, has it that sharks once swam up the river from the sea. Well, thank God, either the legend is false or they've stopped! In this shark-less river, we refreshed our weary bodies, toured the riverbank, and just "limed."

At the end of this synod-type journey, I recalled the story of a student who asked a guru, "Which is more important: the journey or the destination?"

The guru replied, "The company."

Well, the synod journey is also about the COMPANY!

Individual or Group Reflection

MISSIONARY CHALLENGE

At the end of this synod-type journey, I recalled the story of a student who asked a guru, "Which is more important: the journey or the destination?" The guru replied, "The company."

SYNODAL EXERCISE

1. This synod journey allows us the opportunity to share our stories and experiences in the Church and to attentively listen to others' stories. Which currently marginalised group might you want to be your companion on this journey? Why?
2. How is God's presence revealed in this marginalised group?

CHAPTER FORTY-SIX

Synodality Lesson at the Swimming Pool

One morning, I arrived at my swimming class and encountered a new coach. I thought I had erred in the time for my regular class, but was assured I had not. There was a substitute coach for that day.

During the class, I felt more relaxed and confident, less stressed or anxious. I observed that every swimmer, regardless of their competencies, finished routines almost at the same time. The coach waited on weaker swimmers, like me, to complete one routine before giving instructions for the next. And the instructions were clearly communicated so that all the swimmers understood. No one needed ask: "What were the instructions?"

At the end of the class, I shared my observations with the new coach, comparing this approach to that of previous instructors. He said, "Experience teaches coaches the art of carrying the whole group together."

"Wow!" I exclaimed to myself. "**This** is synodality! Carrying the whole group **together**."

Individual or Group Reflection

MISSIONARY CHALLENGE

Experience teaches coaches the art of carrying the whole group together.

SYNODAL EXERCISE

1. The concept of "carrying the whole group together" may sound a bit countercultural, different from practices which may be more prevalent. What competencies would you need to develop to journey together with the "whole group"?
2. What might be your greatest challenges as you journey with the "whole group"?
3. Where in the Scriptures do we encounter Jesus as countercultural?

CHAPTER FORTY-SEVEN

Community

Chapter Sixteen of Joan Chittister's, *The Monastic Heart*, entitled "Community: On Spiritual Companionship", contains a wealth of insights on the communal synodal journey. Excerpts from it are presented in this chapter. Spend some time in reflection on them as a family or group using the *Lectio Divina* method. These guidelines on how to apply *Lectio Divina* can enrich your reflections:

- Begin with an opening prayer, asking for the guidance of the Holy Spirit. Have each person read the quotations aloud, repeating them two or three times. Have each person identify and read aloud the quotation that most strikes them.
- Everyone meditates on the quotations, ponders them, asking themselves: What insights are emerging for me? How can I apply these insights to my life and my community?

- Each person briefly shares their own insights.
- Close with a prayer.

"The truth is that only in community can you come to truly know yourself, as well as grow to the fullness of yourself. It's in community that your intentions, your goals, your gifts, your genuine spiritual depth – and your spiritual immaturity – are exposed and tested and stretched" (p. 83).

"The point is that you come to community to become the best of yourself, which means that the worst of yourself will surely be tempted there" (p. 83).

"The strength of community lies in the differences that diversity offers ... Community becomes the chain that binds the vision together" (p. 84).

"It is exactly the community to which you belong – and the way you belong to it – that will determine what, in the end, becomes of your life. What the community as community believes and does and develops will mold what you really become" (p. 84).

"Community reminds you that the human race cannot possibly thrive unless and until we open our arms to one another" (p. 84).

"Community is clear and living proof that it is precisely diversity that provides the resources needed to bring resilience, creativity, ingenuity, and vision to the task of humanizing humanity" (p. 84).

"We come to community to find the core of life and share it with others. Community is the commitment to carry others through their periods of darkness as they carry us through ours. It is about sustaining others and being sustained when we have gone as far as we can go alone" (p. 83).

Individual or Group Reflection

MISSIONARY CHALLENGE

"The truth is that only in community can you come to truly know yourself, as well as grow to the fullness of yourself. It's in community that your intentions, your goals, your gifts, your genuine spiritual depth – and your spiritual immaturity – are exposed and tested and stretched."

SYNODAL EXERCISE

1. Have you identified a community with which you will you be doing your synodal journey?
2. Why have you selected this community?
3. Pause for a moment and pray for discernment of and alignment with God's will. What emerges for you?

CHAPTER FORTY-EIGHT

Synodality in Action

True to the proverbial saying, "Rome was not built in a day", synodality is not a one-time event. It is a participatory journey that forms a new People of God for mission. In an article by Charles de Pechpeyrou entitled, "'Mama Hekima' Project Empowering Women in DR Congo," I could see synodality in action.

Mama Hekima means "Wisdom Mothers" or "Mothers of Wisdom" in Swahili. The *Mama Hekima* Association aims to bring Kisangani women together to help them become financially independent, notwithstanding their ethnic and religious differences. The Congregation of the Daughters of Wisdom have been managing the project for over ten years. Its founder, Sister Virginie Bitshanda, explained that the women join forces and support each other in dealing with financial hardship, family illness, and ignorance about women's rights.

Among the group's major obstacles were the women's religious and ethnic differences. Catholics, Muslims, Jehovah's Witnesses, Protestants, and Revival Church Christians number among the membership. Sr. Virginie said that "the group asked to be subdivided according to religious denomination. It seemed impossible to these women with so many different faiths to work together".

With the Daughters' dedicated accompaniment, the skills, courage, qualities, and love among the women inspired hope. The Mothers gradually developed harmony among themselves and decided to look beyond their differences. When relational difficulties arose, they chose to cooperate, overcome ethnic and religious differences, and build peace. Sr. Bitshanda said, "On her own, a woman can't do it. ... Instead, united with others, a solution can always be found."

Through the association, the women learned to work together. Depending on their interests, each woman worked in a small group of up to twenty others. Formation focussed on topics such as civic education, women's rights, family planning, managing the family budget and income, and developing tools to increase their economic autonomy. The women have since branched out from growing cassava for domestic use to selling it commercially and to the production of wood stoves.

Consequently, malnutrition and other illnesses were cured, and children were able to go to school, some to university. The women learnt to control their own lives, grew in confidence, and resisted exploitation by the country's unjust systems.

"What a joy it is to see them reap the benefits of this accompaniment," said Sr. Virginie, "which, little by little, helps them not only in their financial support but also to find once more their dignity as 'Mamas.'"

Individual or Group Reflection

MISSIONARY CHALLENGE

"What a joy it is to see them reap the benefits of this accompaniment which, little by little, helps them not only in their financial support but also to find once more their dignity as 'Mamas'."

SYNODAL EXERCISE

1. Consider your community. What common cause could persons be drawn to support, irrespective of their ethnic and religious backgrounds?
2. What might dignity of self and for each other look like as you work together for this common cause?
3. Ask God for guidance as you seek to discern the cause.

CHAPTER FORTY-NINE

A Taste of Perfection, Satisfaction, and Completeness

We don't look for perfection,
    for satisfaction,
    for completeness,

In one
    leaf of a tree,
    blade of grass,
    droplet of water, or
    grain of sand.

Then why do we look for perfection,
    for satisfaction,
    for completeness,

WALKING TOGETHER

In one person,
>	social group,
>	idea,
>	spirituality,
>	religion,
>	political ideology,
>	nuclear family,
>	economic model?

Perfection, satisfaction, completeness
>	are never perfect, satisfied, or complete.

It's like a journey towards the horizon,
>	an imperfect, unsatisfied, and incomplete
>>	journey.

A journey that gives us a taste
of perfection, satisfaction, completeness.
A taste revealed in togetherness, not aloneness.
Like the togetherness of clusters of leaves on a tree,
>	collections of blades of grass,
>	numerous droplets of water,
>	grains of sand.

Perfection, satisfaction, completeness.
We taste it in the diversity of
>	community,

A TASTE OF PERFECTION, SATISFACTION, AND COMPLETENESS

    relationships,
    ideas,
    spiritualities,
    ethnicities and races,
    personalities.

We taste perfection, satisfaction, completeness
    as a human family,
    journeying today in preparation
    for becoming fully perfect, satisfied, and complete
    tomorrow.

Individual or Group Reflection

MISSIONARY CHALLENGE

We taste perfection, satisfaction, completeness as a human family,
> journeying today in preparation
> for becoming fully perfect, satisfied, and complete

tomorrow.

SYNODAL EXERCISE

1. What emotions surface when you consider your own imperfections and those of others?
2. How might the willingness to acknowledge your vulnerabilities and imperfections, and those of others, assist in this journey to perfection, satisfaction, and completeness?
3. "Before I formed you in the womb I knew you; before you were born, I set you apart. I appointed you as a prophet to the nations" (Jeremiah 1:1). How might your knowledge that you were formed in your mother's womb assist on this synodal journey?

CHAPTER FIFTY

Imperfections

Prior to the coronavirus lockdown and restrictions, I celebrated Mass with the Bethesda Catholic Community. This community promotes the inclusion of persons with disabilities into the liturgies by making liturgical spaces sensory-friendly. Children and adults of varying ages and locations on the autistic spectrum were at this Mass; parents or guardians accompanied their children.

Mass was celebrated at the Holy Trinity R.C. Church's spacious and air-conditioned pastoral centre in Arouca, Trinidad and Tobago. Comfortable chairs were placed in a semi-circular position around the altar and at the same level with it. The altar was at the centre.

It was my first time celebrating Mass with persons living with this type of disability. The children's behaviour was aligned to what might be expected of children with autism. Some sat in silence listening attentively, others walked around the liturgical space, while some sat in their chairs with movements difficult to comprehend. One participant came up to me during the homily, gently touched my cheeks, and walked away.

These unusual behaviours agitated, disturbed, discomfited, even disoriented me. I realised these feelings were triggered because I was accustomed to celebrating Masses designed for predictable, controllable behaviour. The liturgy is not sanitised and designed to accommodate persons with disabilities, but so-called "normal" people. Yet, closed-off, sanitised spaces for crying "normal" children are designed.

That occasion with the Bethesda Community moved me to ponder a fundamental synodal question: how do we intentionally include the excluded? Communities such as Bethesda generally do not come into being to help the wider community include the weak. Rather, they develop owing to the wider community's penchant for neglecting weak and vulnerable persons, ignoring their basic human need of belonging.

As we form a synodal Church, the call is not to sanitise the weak and vulnerable who number among the People of God. Nor is it to sanitise our pastoral activities as though human weakness, failures, inadequacies, or imperfections were not a reality.

If God becomes incarnate in the imperfection of human nature as a means of salvation, then a synodal Church is called to immerse itself in the imperfections of its community on its missionary journey.

Individual or Group Reflection

MISSIONARY CHALLENGE

As we form a synodal Church, the call is not to sanitise the weak and vulnerable who number among the People of God. Nor is it to sanitise our pastoral activities as though human weakness, failures, inadequacies, or imperfections were not a reality.

SYNODAL EXERCISE

Prayer:
Heavenly Father, grant me the patience, the wisdom, understanding, and compassion to include, more intentionally, those who are now excluded.

1. Pause for a few moments and create a list of those individuals and groups that you and your community currently exclude.
2. How might you begin to embrace them?

CHAPTER FIFTY-ONE

An Anthropological & Psychological Take on Synodality

John T. Cacioppo, founder of the field of social neuroscience, explains that, anthropologically, humans derive strength from our collective ability to plan, communicate, and work together. This is because our hormonal and genetic makeup support interdependence over independence. He said in a 2013 TEDx Talk: "Whether we know it or not, our brain and biology have been shaped to favor this outcome" (*Dare*, p. 25).

Cacioppo further illuminates how the biological machinery of the brain warns us when our ability to survive and prosper is threatened. Hunger is a warning that our blood sugar is low, for example, and we need to eat. Pain alerts us to potential tissue damage. Loneliness tells us that we need social connection.

Our response to the warning sign of loneliness is to be found in the qualitative, not quantitative, connection of friendships, says Susan Pinker in Brown's *Braving the Wilder-*

ness. Therefore, connection matters, journeying together matters, and synodality matters. We are innately programmed for belonging. It is because we are wired thus that shame is so painful and debilitating, says Brown (*Braving*, pp. 48-49).

Research shows that living with air pollution increases our odds of an early death by five percent. Living with obesity by 20 percent. Excessive drinking: 30 percent. And living with loneliness increases our odds of dying early by 45 percent. In *Let Us Dream*, Pope Francis shares:

> I've experienced three 'Covids' in my own life: my illness, Germany, and Córdoba. When I got really sick at the age of twenty-one, I had my first experience of limit, of pain and loneliness. It changed the way I saw life. ... The serious illness I lived through taught me to depend on the goodness and wisdom of others. (*Dream*, p. 39)

As we journey together, let us think on these insights.

Individual or Group Reflection

MISSIONARY CHALLENGE

We are innately programmed for belonging. It is because we are wired thus that shame is so painful and debilitating.

SYNODAL EXERCISE

1. Are there times when you experience loneliness?
2. Do you willingly reach out to others, or do you hesitate?
3. What might be the cause of your hesitation?
4. Where is God in your loneliness?

CHAPTER FIFTY-TWO

Togetherness

The solar system is a planetary system,
Not 'cause of one planet,
But a diversity of planets.

The beach is the beach,
Not 'cause of one grain of sand,
But diverse sand grains together.

The ocean is the ocean,
Not 'cause of one droplet of water,
But millions of diverse droplets together.

Trees are trees,
Not 'cause of one leaf standing alone,
But scores of diverse leaves together.

WALKING TOGETHER

The forest is the forest,
Not 'cause of one tree standing alone,
But thousands of diverse trees standing together.

A football game is a football game,
Not 'cause of one spectator in a massive stadium,
But thousands of diverse spectators cheering together.

A village is a village,
Not 'cause of one resident,
But a diversity of residents living together.

Language is a language,
Not 'cause of one word,
But together,
Different letters forming different words,
Different words forming different sentences,
Different sentences forming different paragraphs,
Different paragraphs forming different stories.

The Caribbean is the Caribbean.
Not 'cause of one race and creed,
But different races and creeds together,
intermingling,
Forming a hybrid culture.

Togetherness is the God of creation.
Togetherness is the DNA of creation.

TOGETHERNESS

Togetherness is the heartbeat of peoples and cultures.

Togetherness is the engine of Jesus' mission.

Togetherness is the algorithm of the Church's mission.

Togetherness is Synod.

Individual or Group Reflection

MISSIONARY CHALLENGE

"Fostering participation leads us out of ourselves to involve others who hold different views than we do. Listening to those who have the same views as we do bears no fruit. Dialogue involves coming together across diverse opinions. ... Indeed, God often speaks through the voices of those that we can easily exclude, cast aside, or discount." (*Vademecum* 2.2.)

SYNODAL EXERCISE

1. Make a list of individuals or groups who may have opinions that are different to your own.
2. Start a conversation with the individual or a member of one of the groups identified in the previous point. Practise attentive listening.
3. Consider one encounter that Jesus had with a person marginalised by society. What was the quality of His dialogue with them? How does this compare with your completed dialogue?

Conclusion

With multiple responsibilities and seductive attractions demanding our attention, setting aside time to read and reflect in today's busy culture is a challenge. Perhaps you occasionally failed to be faithful, but you never gave up. Thank you for staying the course.

As we conclude this journey, I encourage you to recall some of the vivid, colourful images and metaphors used to capture the meaning of synodality: the People of God walking together to listen, dialogue, and discern. Remember the metaphors of the synodal eye or running? These images are intended to help you connect deeply with the experience of the synod.

As you engaged in the reflection questions, do you recall some of the interior movements, your prevailing feelings? What was resonating deep down in your belly bottom? Some of these interior movements may have been resistance to growth, listening, and dialogue, while others were an invitation to inner transformation, to metamorphosis, like the miraculous transformation of a caterpillar to a colourful butterfly. As we walked together, I invited you to see the interior movements as poking us to listen deeply, calling us to build community despite the resistance.

Both these takeaways are captured in two AEC Synod Synthesis testimonies in preparation for the Synod Assembly 2024. One says: "As Caribbean people, we recognise that it is difficult, a challenge, to stop speaking and just listen to others since we love to speak and communicate." The other testimony reads: "During the dialogue, a community was built!" While these takeaways highlight the challenges of listening and community-building, they are filled with hope that we can grow in these skills.

You would recall that there were significant signposts on the journey. First, the chapters, assigned weekly, that captured aspects of synodality. Then, there were the "Missionary Challenge" sections, the main points of the chapters reminding us that, as the Church, we exist for the mission. Finally, the "Synodal Exercise" sections that, like gym work, challenged us to build synodal memory, the muscles that enable us to walk together.

We are living in a deeply polarised and dysfunctional world. Families, parishes, political parties, and religious groups often yield to the temptation to retreat to their ideological or religious bunkers, firing verbal, sometimes actual, gunshots at perceived opponents. This bunker life results in divisions, violence, and wars both in religious and secular societies. People are labelled as conservative or liberal, but are similar in their resistance to suggestions of sitting around a table to listen, dialogue, and come to consensus. This way of life is opposed to Jesus' mission as reflected in His prayer: "May they all be one as You and I are one" (John 17:21).

Synodality is a spiritual and pastoral pathway to fulfil Jesus' mandate of oneness. It empowers and engages us to hold a healthy tension within complex diversities, leading us to discern the voice of the Holy Spirit because there is: "One Lord, one faith, one baptism. One God and Father of all..." (Ephesians 4:5).

If we are concerned about restoring the Church's unity and witness to society, synodality is a tested and tried spiritual and pastoral approach. The Church has been living this since New Testament times. I take you back to the first Council of Jerusalem (Acts 15) when the opposing voices of Gentile and Jewish Christians threatened the oneness of the early Church. As Acts recalls, the synodal approach, discerning the voice of the Spirit, was the medicine applied to preserve the Church's unity.

As a final inspiration on your journey, I leave you with the Jamaican bus ride as a metaphor for synodality. On a public ride, when the bus departs the terminus, passengers are in unassigned seats. The bus stops periodically along the route, as expected, for passengers to disembark or board. What can be a surprise is the bus stopping to allow far more passengers to board than it seems the bus can accommodate. With each new commuter, the conductor instructs those in the bus: "Small up yourself!" This means make space for the newcomers!

A synod testimony from the Diocese of Cayenne, French Guyana, helps us appreciate this packed bus ride: "Accepting the other in my life can be uncomfortable, but it is a way to become more human. The other takes me out of myself; it opens me to relationship, and God is a relationship."

Taking us out of ourselves is precisely the purpose of synodality so that we become one as we continue walking together on the missionary journey.

Works Cited & Consulted

Bernache, Evan. "The 3 Levels of Conversation." *EB Coaching International*, evanbernache.com/2018/09/26/the-3-levels-of-conversation/.

Brown, Brené. *Braving the Wilderness: The Quest for True Belonging and the Courage to Stand Alone*. Kindle Version. Random House, 2017.

---. *Dare To Lead: Brave Work. Tough Conversations. Whole Hearts*. Kindle Version. Random House, 2018.

---. *Daring Greatly: How the Courage to Be Vulnerable Transforms the Way We Live, Love, Parent, and Lead*. Kindle Version. Avery, 2012.

Cacioppo, John T. "To Grow to Adulthood as a Social Species", *The Lethality of Loneliness*. TEDxDes-Moines transcript, 9 Sep. 2013, singjupost.com/

john-cacioppo-on-the-lethality-of-loneliness-full-transcript/, 7 Mar. 2016.

Chambers, Donald D. "Conversation, Conversation, Conversation." *Beloved Reflections*, 18 Aug. 2021, belovedreflections.org/2021/08/18/conversation-conversation-conversation/.

Chittister, Joan. *Radical Spirit: 12 Ways to Live a Free and Authentic Life*. Convergent Books. 25 Apr. 2017.

---. *The Monastic Heart: 50 Simple Practices for a Contemplative and Fulfilling Life*. Convergent Books, 21 Sep. 2021.

Codina, Victor. "Why Do Some Catholics Oppose Pope Francis?" *America: The Jesuit Review*, 12 Sep. 2019, americamagazine.org/faith/2019/09/12/why-do-some-catholics-oppose-pope-francis.

"Conversational Intelligence." *The Creating WE Institute*, 2024, creatingwe.com/benchmark/conversational-intelligence.

De Pechpeyrou, Charles. "'Mama Hekima' Project Empowering Women in DR Congo." *Vatican News*, 2 Sep. 2022, vaticannews.va/en/church/news/2022-09/sisters-project-mama-hekima-virginie-bitshanda-dr-congo.html.

Dodd, Liz. "Lay Catholics Condemn Bishops' Synodal Process." *The Tablet*, 12 Aug. 2021, thetablet.co.uk/news/14388/lay-catholics-condemn-bishops-synodal-process.

"Father General Arturo Sosa, S.J.: Taking the Risk – Making Discernment Central." *Discerning Leadership*, Discerning Leadership Programme, 28 Oct. 2019, discerningleadership.org/releases/father-general-arturo-sosa-s-j-taking-the-risk-making-discernment-central/.

"Forever Young." Alphaville. *YouTube,* uploaded by Cappew22, 00.57-1.02, 9 Mar. 2009, youtube.com/watch?v=t1TcDHrkQYg&t=53s.

Francis. "Audience with the Members of the International Theological Commission." Address. *The Holy See*, Rome, 29 Nov. 2019, press.vatican.va/content/salastampa/en/bollettino/pubblico/2019/11/29/191129b.html.

---. "Evangelii Gaudium" (The Joy of the Gospel). Apostolic Exhortation. *The Holy See*, 24 Nov. 2013, vatican.va/content/francesco/en/apost_exhortations/documents/papa-francesco_esortazione-ap_20131124_evangelii-gaudium.html.

---. "Free Thought: Morning Meditation in the Chapel of the Domus Sanctae Marthae." Daily Meditation. *Dicastero per la Comunicazione – Libreria Editrice Vaticana*, Rome, 29 Nov. 2013, vatican.va/content/francesco/en/cotidie/2013/documents/papa-francesco-cotidie_20131129_free-thought.html.

---. "Listening with the Ear of the Heart – 56th World Day of Social Communications." Message. *The Holy See*, Rome, 24 Jan. 2022, vatican.va/content/francesco/en/

messages/communications/documents/20220124-messaggio-comunicazioni-sociali.html#_ftnref2.

Francis and Ivereigh, Austen. *Let Us Dream: The Path to a Better Future.* Kindle Version. Simon and Schuster, 2024.

Frankel, Estelle. *The Wisdom of Not Knowing: Discovering a Life of Wonder by Embracing Uncertainty.* Kindle Version. Shambhala, 2017.

Frost, Michael. "The Lonely Crowd: Churches Dying Due to Friendlessness." *Mike Frost.* 22 July 2020, mikefrost.net/the-lonely-crowd-churches-dying-due-to-friendlessness/.

Gordon, Charles Jason. *Reviving Our Caribbean Soul: A Contemplative Synodal Journey.* 6 June 2024.

Holt-Lunstad, J., M. Baker, T. Harris, D. Stephenson, and T.B. Smith. "Loneliness and Social Isolation as Risk Factors for Mortality: A Meta-Analytic Review." *Perspectives on Psychological Science*, 10(2), 2015, 227-37).

"Jerusalem Bible." *Jerusalem Bible Online*, 2016, bibletold.com.

John Paul. "Catechesi Tradendae (On Catechesis in Our Time)." Apostolic Exhortation. *The Holy See*, Rome, 16 Oct. 1979, vatican.va/content/john-paul-ii/en/apost_exhortations/documents/hf_jp-ii_exh_16101979_catechesi-tradendae.html.

Jung, Carl. *Alchemical Studies.* Princeton University Press, 1967.

Kelly, Matthew. *Rediscover the Saints: Twenty-Five Questions That Will Change Your Life*. Kindle Version. Blue Sparrow, 2019.

Latin American Episcopal Conference CELAM and Bergoglio, Jorge Mario. "The Aparecida Document – Fifth General Conference of the Bishops of Latin America and the Caribbean." *CELAM*, 5 Aug. 2013, celam.org/aparecida/Ingles.pdf.

Luciani, Rafael. *Synodality: A New Way of Proceeding in the Church*. Paulist Press, New York, 2022.

MacQuarrie, John. *Existentialism*. Westminster, Philadelphia, PA, 1972.

New King James Version (NKJV). *Bible Gateway*, HarperCollins Christian Publishing, biblegateway.com.

Patrignani, Adélaïde. "Sister Becquart: There is No Synodality Without Spirituality." *Vatican News*, 23 July 2021, vaticannews.va/en/vatican-city/news/2021-07/nathalie-becquart-synod-bishops-interview-synodality-spiritualit.html.

Paul VI. "Dogmatic Constitution on Divine Revelation – Dei Verbum (Word of God)." *The Holy See*, Rome, 18 Nov. 1965, vatican.va/archive/hist_councils/ii_vatican_council/documents/vat-ii_const_19651118_dei-verbum_en.html#.

---. "Dogmatic Constitution on the Church – Lumen Gentium (Light of the Nations)." *The Holy See*, Rome, 21 Nov. 1964, vatican.va/archive/hist_councils/ii_vatican_council/documents/vat-ii_const_19641121_lumen-gentium_en.html.

---. "Pastoral Constitution on the Church in the Modern World – Gaudium et Spes." *The Holy See*, Rome, 7 Dec. 1965, vatican.va/archive/hist_councils/ii_vatican_council/documents/vat-ii_const_19651207_gaudium-et-spes_en.html.

Rohr, Richard. *Everything Belongs: The Gift of Contemplative Prayer*. Revised ed. Crossroad Publishing, New York, 2003.

---. *Job and the Mystery of Suffering: Spiritual Reflections*. Kindle Version. The Crossroad Publishing Company, NY, 2020.

"Sensus Fidei in the Life of the Church." International Theological Commission. *Vatican: The Holy See*. Rome, 2014, vatican.va/roman_curia/congregations/cfaith/cti_documents/rc_cti_20140610_sensus-fidei_en.html.

"Synodality in the Life and Mission of the Church." International Theological Commission. *Vatican: The Holy See*. Rome, 2 Mar. 2018, vatican.va/roman_curia/congregations/cfaith/cti_documents/rc_cti_20180302_sinodalita_en.html#.

"The Preparatory Document – For a Synodal Church: Communion, Participation, and Mission." Synod of Bishops. *Libreria Editrice Vaticana*, Vatican City, Rome, 7 Sep. 2021, synod.va/en/news/the-preparatory-document.html.

Tornielli, Andrea. "Cardinal Grech: The Church is Synodal Because it is a Communion." *Vatican News*, 21 July 2021, vaticannews.va/en/vatican-city/news/2021-07/cardinal-grech-synod-synodality-interview-communion.html.

"Vademecum for the Synod on Synodality: Official Handbook for Listening and Discernment in Local Churches." Secretary General of the Synod of Bishops. *Vatican City*, Rome, Sep. 2021, synod.va/content/dam/synod/document/common/vademecum/Vademecum-EN-A4.pdf.

Watkins, Devin. "Pope at Audience: 'Old Age is Where Wisdom is Woven'." *Vatican News*, 24 Aug. 2022, vaticannews.va/en/pope/news/2022-08/pope-francis-general-audience-old-age-death-childbirth.html.

Wilson, George. "Stage One of the Synod: Listening to the Faithful." *La Croix International*, 16 June 2021, international.la-croix.com/news/religion/stage-one-of-the-synod-listening-to-the-faithful/14481.

Wooden, Cindy. "Not a Walk in the Park: Synod Journey Requires Listening, Patience." *Crux*. 30 May 2021, cruxnow.com/vatican/2021/05/not-a-walk-in-the-park-synod-journey-requires-listening-patience.

---. "Synod Process Must Begin 'From Bottom Up', Pope Tells Bishops." *National Catholic Reporter*, 25 May 2021, ncronline.org/vatican/synod-process-must-begin-bottom-pope-tells-bishops#:~:text.

About the Authors

Father Donald D. Chambers is a Roman Catholic priest of the Archdiocese of Kingston, Jamaica. He is the General Secretary of the Antilles Episcopal Conference and currently serves as Facilitator of the Synod Process for that organisation. A lecturer in theology at the Seminary of St. John Vianney and the Uganda Martyrs in Trinidad and Tobago, he is an active member of the Conference on Theology in the Caribbean Today.

Fr. Donald is a frequent contributor on the theme of synodality to the *Catholic News* (Trinidad and Tobago), the *Catholic Opinion* (Jamaica), and the *Catholic Standard* (Guyana). He has contributed to festschrift publications for various scholars and has authored *Justice and Peace in a*

Renewed Caribbean: Contemporary Catholic Reflections (2012) with Anna Kasafi Perkins and Jacqueline Porter, *Transformed by the Deep: Reflections of a Caribbean Priest* (2017), and *From Exile to Inner Peace: The Journey of a Caribbean Priest* (2022). See more of Fr. Donald's work at *belovedreflections.org*.

Judy Joseph McSween is a Certified Coach and Trainer in the areas of Emotional, Conversational, and Spiritual Intelligence. For over fifteen years, she has been actively engaged in facilitating the ongoing formation of the laity and ordained in faith-based organisations. Her passion for working with these emerged during her introduction to Christian Meditation practice and parallel certification as an Organisation Development Facilitator. It stemmed from her own unease in integrating spirituality in all dimensions of her life. As this unease diminished, her fervour for working with others to achieve the same soared.

Judy currently serves in the Archdiocese of Port of Spain on the Diocesan Animation Team and the Seminary Human Formation Team at the Seminary of St. John Vianney and the Uganda Martyrs. She also facilitates Emotional Intelligence and Spirituality, Conversations in the Spirit, Spiritual Listening, and Christian Meditation programmes. She has conducted retreats and workshops in dioceses within the Antilles Episcopal Conference and for various religious denominations in Trinidad and Tobago, St. Vincent and the

ABOUT THE AUTHORS

Grenadines, the US Virgin Islands, the USA, and Canada. For more on Judy's work, visit *www.timeoutspecialist.com*.

Made in the USA
Columbia, SC
10 December 2024